# THE DRESSAGE **SEAT**

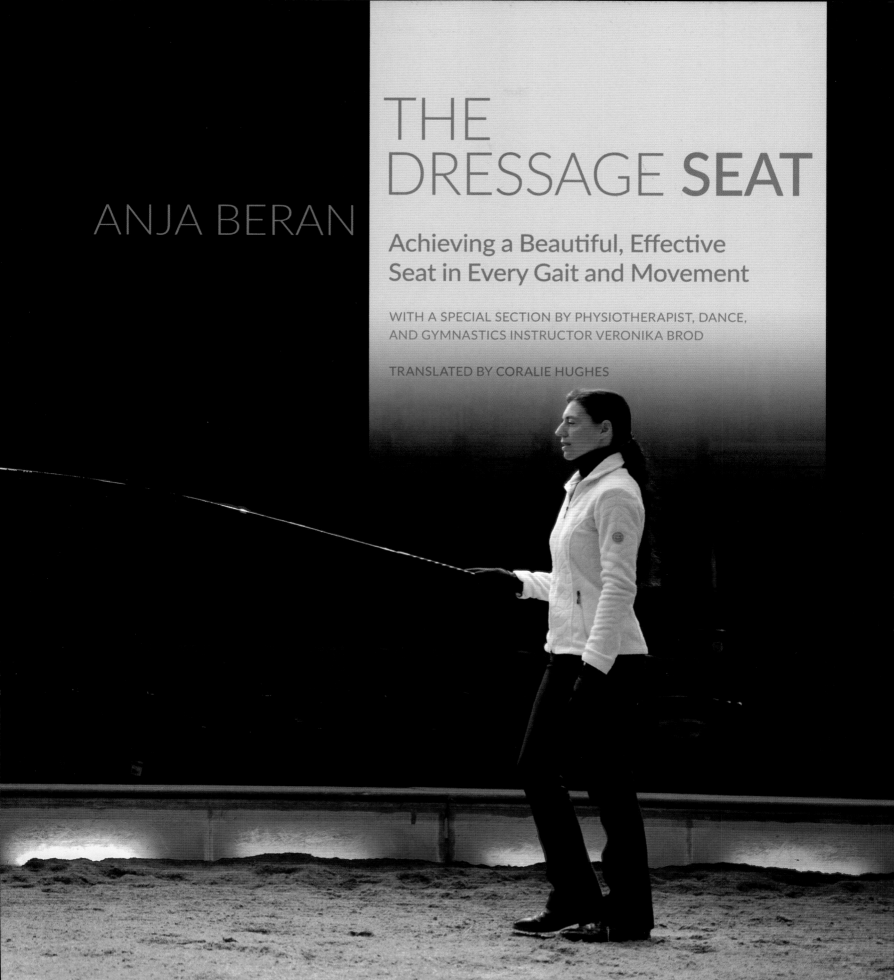

ANJA BERAN

# THE
# DRESSAGE SEAT

Achieving a Beautiful, Effective
Seat in Every Gait and Movement

WITH A SPECIAL SECTION BY PHYSIOTHERAPIST, DANCE,
AND GYMNASTICS INSTRUCTOR VERONIKA BROD

TRANSLATED BY CORALIE HUGHES

First published in the United States of America in 2017 by
Trafalgar Square Books
North Pomfret, Vermont 05053

Originally published in the German language as *Der Dressursitz* by Crystal Verlag, Wentorf

Library of Congress Control Number: 2017933884
ISBN: 9781570767937

Photos by Maresa Mader except pp. 80, 121 (Michael Poganiatz)

Illustrations by Susanne Retsch-Amschler (pp. 10, 84–90, 104, 106, 107, 110, 111, 113, 118, 126, 128, 130) and Cornelia Koller (pp. 7, 12, 54, 57, 59)

Interior design by Alessandra Kreibaum
Cover design by RM Didier
Index by Andrea Jones (JonesLiteraryServices.com)
Printed in China

10 9 8 7 6 5 4 3 2 1

# CONTENTS

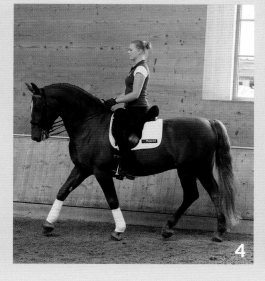

70

74

82

102

146

Translator's note: For clarity of meaning, we have followed the convention of referring to riders as "she" and horses as "he." We fully appreciate the gentlemen riders and the mares!

# INTRODUCTION TO **PART ONE**

*"The most important element that makes the separate entities of horse and rider into one unit, allows the rider to control the animal, and gives the horse self-carriage and movement that make him whole, is the seat."*

–Gustav von Dreyhausen   *Die Reitkunst im Spiegel ihrer Meister* (The art of riding as seen through its masters) by Bertold Schirg (Olms Verlag, 1987)

*The aids can only be given lightly and in harmony when the seat is well trained. Anja Beran on the Lipizzaner stallion Favory Toscana.*

The most important job of a good seat is not to disturb the horse. A seat that isn't quiet and symmetrical can lead to great discomfort, even pain, and ultimately can get in the way of the horse's even and free movement. Being ridden for a long time by a rider with a bad seat can also lead to negative tension and health issues.

When the rider has developed a seat that can harmoniously follow the horse's movement, the next step is to learn to aid effectively to develop him. Harmony with the horse and the animal's motivation are strongly dependent on a supple and effective seat.

The seat has always played a large role in my instruction to help and protect the horse from a rider who sits crookedly or too heavily. Over the years, I have learned that I can't be successful at teaching with mere "rider commands and tips" since more and more people are starting to ride later in life. How I approach teaching the seat is difficult. I can best help the student when I have clear images and deep knowledge. Experience has taught me to think about the rider from four different points of view to more effectively help her improve. The perspectives are:

1. Technical training by a riding instructor to teach the seat and to help the student develop "feel" when riding.

2. Assistance from a physiotherapist to improve posture, movement, body awareness, coordination, stability, and mobility.

3. Control of breathing to assure an even flow of breath despite concentrating on other things.

4. The psychological aspect, because a good ride begins in the head.

I can only help the rider sufficiently when I think about the seat from different perspectives. There isn't any new knowledge about how to sit a horse well, but sometimes a special tip or a good visual can help you use your body in a different way. Understanding why you can't do it, or why you sit in some particular way, can help you make great progress.

Perhaps you have previously only addressed the symptoms?

A good seat requires the constant pursuit of improvement. Anjan Beran on the Lusitano stallion Campeao.

You shouldn't simply accept deficiencies in your seat: it should always be your intention to improve it. The longer I work with horses the clearer it is: the problem—almost always—is sitting in the saddle!

As Otto de la Croix said, out of respect and for the good of the horse, the seat deserves the greatest attention:

*"Everything depends on the seat. It engages the back of the horse, thereby organizing—or weakening—the large connecting link between the hindquarters and the front of the horse. The effect of the seat impacts incontrovertible laws of nature. The seat aids are there to be used whenever the rider is in the saddle, and when subtle and nuanced, be understood by even the most resistant horses."*

Die Reitkunst im Spiegel ihrer Meister (The art of riding as seen through its masters) by Bertold Schirg (Olms Verlag, 1987)

# THE DRESSAGE SEAT

## FROM THE RIDER'S POINT OF VIEW

### Physical Requirements That Make Riding Easier

#### Anatomy

There are people who find it is easier to sit well on a horse simply because of their anatomy. Body size is an important factor. Someone who is very small with short legs that barely hang down the saddle panels has a hard time using her legs and would have an especially hard time on a very large horse. On the other hand, very large riders often have a problem balancing. On many horses, their legs hang far below the body of the horse, and they can get used to wrapping their legs around the horse or pulling their legs up when trying to aid effectively. The ideal rider is of medium size with relatively long legs and an upper body that isn't too tall. Flat thighs make positioning the legs easier. Very round thighs make it more difficult to let the legs hang loose on the horse and a tendency to not sit well on the seat while carrying the weight more on the thighs.

A symmetrical build is a gift for a beginning rider. Relaxed shoulders that are held precisely over a horizontal pelvis lead to symmetrical leg length. This is ideal for being able to sit in balance on a horse. Anyone that naturally has an erect posture with shoulders falling loosely back and down, and carries her head straight above a correctly formed vertebral column, is built to ride. Having a solid abdominal and back musculature in an athletic build also makes it easier to learn to ride. Both a hollow lower back, or a rounded back, make it difficult to sit straight on a horse. Anyone with pathological scoliosis of the vertebral column must develop good muscles and should invest in a lot of physiotherapy to be able to sit well on a horse.

A supple pelvis makes it easier for the rider to get into the movement of the horse, and supple ankles make it easier to carry the toes parallel to the horse's body with an elastic spring action.

#### Physical Capabilities

Many people have a natural balance between *mobility* and *stability*. This means that they have sufficient positive tension and muscle

*Someone who is athletic with a naturally straight and erect posture, combined with good body awareness, has the ideal prerequisites to learn to ride well.*

tone while being mobile enough to move with the horse. This is a great advantage to riding well. There are also people who are extremely supple but with very weak muscle tone. These people have a hard time being stable and straight on the horse. They collapse and tend to fall to one side or the other—or forward or backward. In short, they can't carry themselves straight because they are hypermobile. Such people need exercises to build muscle and stability. There is also a group of people who are very stiff with very high muscle tension. These riders have a hard time melting into the movement of the horse and they tend to sit on top of the horse as a "foreign body" without any elasticity.

Being objective about your body awareness is a big advantage because you can notice the mistakes in your posture and concentrate on them. Most of us have many errors of posture or body movement that we aren't aware of, and we can't become aware of them without outside help.

Ultimately, bad posture and an unhealthy way of moving affect our coordination. We need to be able to control our bodies and use individual body parts independently from others. Body awareness and coordination are capabilities that you can develop when young, and they are useful for your whole life. You can best develop these talents in ballet or dance training. Constantly correcting posture in front of a mirror and practicing different steps and ways of moving without losing good posture is very close to what you have to do in the saddle.

Someone in good condition can work at a higher level of effort during a riding lesson than someone who is in poor condition.

Riding without a great expenditure of energy and with fine aids requires a certain level of fitness because the movements of the horse make riding a demanding physical exercise.

It also seems important to me that a rider should know her physical condition well, and consciously use her body accordingly. For example, a heavier rider on a rather small horse should move carefully since her body mass has a big effect with a small amount of effort. On the other hand, someone weighing a mere 110 pounds riding a very large, heavy horse will have to use the seat clearly in order to have an aid be understood.

# How to Use Your Body

## Head, Neck, and Eyes

*"The head must be carried freely, securely, and comfortably. Free so that it follows all the natural movements of riding and able to turn to one side or the other. Secure meaning straight, without tilting to the left or right, forward or back. The head must be carried comfortably because otherwise stiffness will develop that will affect the entire trunk, especially the spine."*
—Claude Bourgelat

*Die Reitkunst im Spiegel ihrer Meister* (The art of riding as seen through its masters) by Bertold Schirg (Olms Verlag, 1987)

Carrying the head freely at the end of the spine requires good neck muscles. At no time should the head wiggle in sync with the movement of the horse. This happens when the rider is blocked in the pelvis, which stiffens the back: the movement of the horse can be seen in the head movement of the rider, because the area where the movement should flow through, namely the pelvis, is blocked. Weak muscles also cause the head to bob. In this case the rider is not able to carry her head. Another bad error is when the head and neck stretches forward. This causes a great deal of tension in the shoulder and neck muscles of the rider. The tension then translates to the whole back. All who ride with this "vulture neck" should think about whether they tend to carry the head forward in their daily life. Usually this posture occurs all the time and can be corrected from the ground (not just when mounted) to the great benefit of the person. As a corrective, you should constantly tell yourself: Chin in! Just as Oeynhausen remarked:

*"The head should be carried up and freely with the chin pulled in. Pulling the chin in helps the whole back. Allowing the head to go forward leads to rounding the back."*

*Die Reitkunst im Spiegel ihrer Meister* (The art of riding as seen through its masters) by Bertold Schirg (Olms Verlag, 1987)

The head should also not hang down. This often happens when the rider focuses her eyes on the horse's neck. It is better to look between the horse's ears in the direction you want to ride. Usually, it is not just the eyes and the head that hang forward and down, but the shoulders also. Like the domino principle, a mistake high up causes negative effects to the rider's entire posture.

Many riders tend to exaggerate when they look in the direction of the turn they want to ride. For example, when they want to turn

left, they don't look (as they should) between the horse's ears through to the left, but rather almost over the inside shoulder to the left and down. This causes their whole body to turn and their shoulders are no longer in sync with the horse's shoulders. Their upper body is turned far too much.

Another frequently seen error is carrying the head to one side. Many riders do this unconsciously and they have to be told over and over so that they can perceive the error. The tendency to carry the head to one side usually involves asymmetry of the shoulders, which leads to collapsing at the waist. Once again we see the chain reaction that results in poor posture throughout the whole body.

There are riders who tend to stick their chin up and out when they transition into a faster gait—the trot or the canter. It looks as if they want to pull themselves into the new gait with their chin. This is a deadly error because their chest also goes forward, the ribs open, the back is likely to hollow, and the rider leans forward out of the saddle so she can no longer effectively use the seat in the up transition.

*Avoid the so-called "vulture neck" where the head is carried forward with very tight neck muscles.*

## The Shoulders and the Arms

### The Shoulders

Ideally, a rider's shoulders should be absolutely symmetrical. You should seek the help of a physiotherapist for this. If there is crookedness, there are gymnastic exercises for improving it. Moreover, the shoulders, in a supple manner, should fall back and down. If you stand sideways in front of a mirror, you can check the position of your shoulders yourself. Even an untrained observer can tell if they are pushed forward or pulled up. There are many gymnastic exercises that can help you improve the position of your shoulders. Imagine shoving your shoulder blades into your back pockets without hollowing your lower back. Shoulders that hang forward can be corrected by lifting the sternum and taking it forward. If the shoulders are pulled up, I recommend lifting the shoulders up even more, and then letting them drop so that you can feel a difference and be more conscious of them.

### The Upper Arms, Elbows, and Lower Arms

The arms should hang down loosely. It is not required to have a 90-degree angle from the upper arm through the elbow to the lower arm: the forearm should fall down in a relaxed way. Elbows that stick out to the side change the position of the shoulders and lead to stiff hands. It is better when they lie softly at the sides of the body without pressure. It is a bad habit to pull the elbows back so that they are behind the upper body. This causes a hollow back and indicates a backward working hand. Many riders stretch their arms forward too much, which brings the elbows forward. They believe that by doing this they are being soft by yielding the hand in the direction of the horse's mouth. This is, however, not the case, because the arms are very stiff in this position and subsequently it is not possible to give aids with feeling. Riders carrying their arms like this tend to ride with the reins much too short. Reins that are a little longer allow the rider to get into a more comfortable position and relax the arms.

### The Wrists and Fingers

The wrist should be turned so that the rider can see her thumbs and not the back of the hand or the fingers. There should be a straight line from the elbow through the wrist so that the wrist is more mobile and supple. When the wrist is cocked to the outside or inside, it is fixed in place and cannot give sensitive aids.

The fingers should be loosely closed in a fist, but never pressed together. Like a pianist, only relaxed fingers can work with softness independently of each other and communicate with the mouth of a horse. It is most important when riding with a curb bit on a horse trained to a higher level that you don't use your arms or wrists. Only a soft subtle movement of the fingers on the bit in the horse's mouth is an aid. The thumb should rest like a little roof over the pointing finger and should be neither pressed down nor stuck out.

Take the whip test: When you are riding with a whip, it should rest lightly across your thigh. If it is directed vertically down the horse's shoulder, your wrist is in an incorrect position, likewise when the point of the whip is up or the whip is placed at your waist. You can tell by the position of the whip if your hand position is correct.

If you want to be a rider who can control her horse with lightness and fine aids, perfect relaxation is very important for your shoulders, arms, and fingers. Any stiffness or muscle tension in this region transfers to the horse's mouth and the horse can react with heaviness and hardness. It is not so hard to let go in this region; you only have to think about it. The problem that gets to many riders is that a good rider needs positive tension in her core to maintain her posture and to ride the horse with her seat. A supple shoulder and arm position with a stable trunk posture is very difficult for many people to develop, because either it is all loose and very mobile, or the trunk tenses with the shoulders and arms.

A good gymnastics teacher can help train this capability outside of the riding lesson. Dancing is also excellent for improving this problem, because there is a regular transition between looseness and tension, and between mobility and stability.

*Correct position of the shoulders—not pulled up but symmetrical with soft arms that hang down. Jana Lacey-Krone on the Lusitano stallion Ramzes at the canter.*

## The Upper Body: The Upper Part of the Trunk

### The Sternum

*An erect posture with relaxed arms and upper legs: Anja Beran on Favory Toscana.*

When you draw the sternum (breastbone) in, it leads to a stiff, round carriage of the upper body, and it is impossible to be straight and relaxed. Since you want your horse to be "up" in front, you must first elevate yourself. This begins with lifting the sternum and bringing it forward. But caution! Many people tend to hollow their back or open their ribs too much and stick the belly forward. In front of a mirror, carefully practice being able to independently bring the sternum forward.

Later, it becomes very important to be able to direct riding movements. For example, in the transition from piaffe to passage, it is ideal when you are able to bring your sternum a little forward to introduce the transition.

### The Ribs

The ribs must be closed. Many people have no idea about whether their ribs are open or closed, but this can be taught. An open rib cage removes many possibilities for using your seat as an aid because it leads to a hollow back. Open ribs also lead to pushing the abdomen forward. This is not just unattractive when riding, it is also not effective. But how do you actively close your ribs? It is best to practice this in good gymnastic or dance lessons in front of a mirror. Imagine that you are about to sneeze. In the moment when you sneeze, you close your ribs. It is not the moment of "Aaaa..." but the moment of "choooo." To feel what is happening to your ribs in this moment, lay your hand on them and try to intentionally make this movement even without sneezing. Closed ribs make for a straight silhouette and help you find a more stable trunk position from which you can effectively influence the horse.

### The Abdomen and the Navel

The abdomen should not be stretched forward because this can cause you to hollow your lower back. Pulling the abdomen in is also a significant mistake because it rounds your back. The abdomen should be stable with positive tension and help hold you erect. The abdominal muscles give your trunk stability, and it is very important that they are well trained. Along with the back muscles, they hold the rider straight. These two muscle regions help you to hold the spine straight and should work together in harmony. When one is very strong and the other too weak, you must work with a good trainer to get symmetrical development of the musculature. Otherwise it is as if a bridge is fastened only on one side with no support on the other. Over time, this is bad for your spine and posture.

Sometimes, we see riders at the sitting trot that have a wave traveling through their whole upper body with every trot step. These riders have stomach muscles that are too weak and have no stability. This instability makes it impossible to effectively give seat aids in, for example, transitions. They have to rely on their hand and leg aids.

The navel is a good posture correction point for the abdomen. According to the error or problem, you can tell the rider to pull the navel in or to stick it out a little.

*You can understand "open ribs" from sneezing: the ribs are wide open during the "aaaa..." and closed during the "...choo," which makes erect posture possible.*

Interestingly, most people are conscious of their navel and can actively direct it. For example, to indicate many movements like the piaffe, it is helpful to bring the navel forward. This can save the rider a lot of leg.

## The Back

An erect posture of the upper body is not just healthy for your back when riding, it should become a habit in daily life. Anyone who strengthens her back musculature and goes through life in an erect posture will protect her vertebral column and vertebral discs. In addition, she will gain a self-confident air that will be profitable in many areas of life. This shows once again how learning to ride well can influence your whole life and help you bring body and mind into sync. The person who has a natural erect posture has it easier finding the correct position in the saddle than one who tends to go through life with a rounded back. Moreover, a straight back makes it easier to ride a horse on the aids. Sitting on the horse with a rounded back robs you of the essential influence of the seat, leaving you with only your legs to ride a horse "forward."

Many riders sense they aren't straight and lean back in the erroneous belief that they can correct their posture in this way.

*Note: The rider, like the horse, should never come behind the vertical!*

Try to get into an erect posture by imagining that you are growing taller and straightening the back, vertebra by vertebra.

*In this half-pass, you can easily see the straight upper body of the rider. Her shoulders are parallel to the ground and there isn't any collapsing at the waist. Silvia Wimmer on the gelding Generale Cassa.*

## The Upper Body:
## The Lower Part of the Trunk

### The Pelvis and the Hip Joints

In order to be able to comfortably sit in the saddle, you should open the pelvis. As soon as the horse begins to move, it is your pelvis that must be extremely mobile in order to follow the movements of the horse. A hollow back will lock your pelvis and you can no longer swing with the horse. You should also not shove your pelvis forward to catch the movement of the horse because this puts your upper body in a backward position and you will sit behind the movement.

Imagine that between the pelvis and the rest of your upper body there is a joint that allows you to move your pelvis independently from the upper body. This is a huge issue for many riders because they are not able to separate the movements of the pelvis from the rest of the body. This leads to an unattractive look, because the whole trunk is like a solid block in movement and, for the horse, this means that he has to carry a huge, stiff object on his back. The rider's pelvis must not only move forward and backward, but also be mobile sideways in every direction. Stiffness in the pelvis can usually be improved through gymnastics and dancing.

The rider's hip joints should be freely mobile. On one hand, this is an important anatomical requirement. On the other hand, choosing the correct saddle can maintain this mobility, because some saddles block the rider in the hip joint. These are saddles with seats that are too narrow and knee blocks that are too big. Many riders actually feel good in them because the blocks give them a false sense of security and a stable position, but what they don't realize is that these saddles constrict, lead to tension, and limit the free movement of the leg from front to back. This free swing of the leg from the hip joint must be possible in a dressage saddle otherwise you cannot give correct and sensitive aids.

When the saddle restricts you, and you want to aid with your legs, you will bend at the knee and pull the leg back and up. This puts your heel, and with it the spur, near the saddle blanket, which is a particularly bad place to try to positively influence a horse: his ears will go back, the neck lifts, and his tail whips around as he signals that he doesn't want to be touched there. So, in order to give fine aids, you need a long, loose leg that can influence from as far down as possible near the girth. The prerequisite for this is a freely functioning hip joint.

### The Seat

This is what you sit on, as relaxed as possible. This means that you shouldn't tense the seat muscles because it pushes you out of the saddle and is also uncomfortable. Many riders are able to sit at the walk with loose seat muscles, however, at the trot, they don't try to follow the movement of the horse, but rather, unconsciously, try to avoid or fight against the movement and tense their seat muscles. It is important to control this and to accept and go along with what the horse gives you, instead of tensing against it. Thinking correctly can help you better control your body.

Sitting equally on both sides of the seat is mandatory if you don't want to cause the horse constant pain. Tension in the horse due to uneven loading is very common. Consequently, regularly have a riding instructor check that you are sitting in the middle. If you have to go a long time without a riding instructor, a good saddler can also check your saddle: when the stuffing is always squashed on the same side, it is likely that you are sitting and loading the saddle crookedly on one side and, of course, the horse, as well. You should definitely have a physiotherapist check your body for symmetry.

*Try to sit in the saddle "broad in the pelvis" and in a relaxed way, covering as much saddle surface area as possible—like a pancake that spreads out onto the whole pan!*

It is important to sit with your seat in the saddle's center of gravity. The center of gravity of the saddle must fit the horse's back, which is the job of the saddle fitter. Usually, it is easy to sit directly on this spot. Problems arise when the saddle doesn't fit the rider. Small riders can sit in different places, and when the saddle is too big, she "swims" in it and slides around. Such an unstable seat understandably upsets the horse in his back, and causes tension.

A very large and heavy rider will feel restricted in a saddle that is too small and her weight can't be well distributed. She is compromised as she sits on this surface that is too small. Sometimes a part of her seat is on areas of the saddle where it shouldn't be. Poor distribution of the rider's weight on the

*An erect posture with a straight waist:
Jana Lacey-Krone on P.R.E. stallion
Maestro in the piaffe.*

back of the horse can cause him tension and disturb his freedom of movement.

An incorrectly tipped pelvis leads to your seat being either too far back toward the cantle or not being properly used because you are in a fork seat. Since the various parts of the body are all interconnected, a mistake seldom has an isolated effect but always influences other body parts.

### The Waist

You must be absolutely straight in the waist. The frequently used command, "Don't drop the hip," actually means bending at the waist.

This leads to a crooked upper body and your weight is not evenly distributed on the saddle. Often, bending at the waist causes the legs to lie in different places on the horse.

Many riders can stay symmetrical and straight in the waist on straight lines, but have trouble when riding curves. They try to follow the bend too much and lean in on the curve by bending in at the inside waist. Simply turning the upper body is sufficient to show the horse the way. Looking between the horse's ears can help you keep yourself straight. You should never look down to the inside—this makes the mistake worse.

Walking the arena figures on foot can help you learn correct posture and how the horse must do it. Turning your trunk without dropping sideways should be your focus.

Lateral movements are another large source of mistakes involving collapsing at the waist. Most riders tend to lean from the waist in the direction of bend. In a left shoulder-in, it is the left side of your waist, and in a half-pass to the right, it is the right side that you must pay attention to. Once again, in this dry run, it is helpful to walk the lateral movements to study correct body posture along with the aids.

## Summary of Upper Body and Pelvis

*"Stable above, mobile below,"* goes the saying for a good rider. This separation of a stable upper body and a mobile pelvis is easy for some people to do while others have huge problems with it. As I've mentioned, gymnastics and dance can help to educate body awareness and coordination to achieve the desired stability and mobility.

The upper body can be described as a stable box (out of which come arms and legs), and that ends in a mobile pelvis. The extremities can be used as necessary and coordinated by the rider. The "box," with the shoulders over the hips, is the center of all activities that make a rider. Arms and legs are necessary accessories, but their use should be reduced as the influence of the "box" increases.

As Udo Bürger wrote:

*"Leaning forward or collapsing forward with an upper body that can't support itself is an inexcusable limpness in the rider that puts the whole weight of this unstable upper body on the forehand with every step. The horse is overloaded and forced to rush. Even the rider's head jutting out forward throws many kilos of weight on the horse at the poll. Consequently, no one riding in an incorrect canter or jumping seat should wonder why the horse goes against the hand, gets too fast or, on the other hand, rolls behind the bit and holds himself back in the gait. Riding forward is regulated by the seat, simply by the rider knowing how to use her own weight."*

The Way to Perfect Horsemanship by Udo Bürger (Trafalgar Square Books, 2012)

## The Leg

In riding, we speak of the leg in three parts: the upper leg (thigh), the knee, and the lower leg. The ankles and toes require a separate discussion.

### The Upper Leg

The flatter the thigh, the easier it is for the rider to place it loosely but correctly against the saddle. The less fearful and more relaxed the rider is, the more relaxed this part of the leg is, because fearful riders tend to grip the saddle with the thigh. You can see the influence that mental factors have on the seat! Consequently, purely technical discussions about how to sit on a horse are insufficient.

The thigh should lie long and flat against the horse. At the beginning of the lesson, I often have my student take both feet out of the stirrups and bring the inside of both thighs away from the saddle. This pulls a little and the rider usually can't hold it for long, but it should be repeated several times until the leg hangs more loosely against the horse's body. After multiple repetitions of this exercise, I have the student pick up the stirrups again, but now, she should feel shorter than before—a good sign. This exercise stretches the muscles and gives the rider a longer leg.

The thigh should not be used to hang on to the horse or to support the weight of the rider, which actually belongs on the saddle. This means you should not sit more on the thighs than the seat because that takes away the ability to use the seat as an aid.

### The Knee

It is a similar situation with the knees because many fearful riders grip with them. In jumping or the posting trot the knees have a special role because they allow standing up—but not in a dressage seat. In the dressage seat, you should have the knees deep and relaxed against the saddle, without any pressure. Gripping with the knees pushes the rider up out of the saddle and she can't follow the movement of the horse with suppleness.

*Knees loose and down—
so goes the motto.*

If you can't manage to keep pushing your knees down and you let them drift up and forward, you will end up in a chair seat. This changes the whole position of the leg, and correct leg aids are no longer possible.

In dressage, we also don't want the knees to stick out with a loosely swinging leg. This is very common. The student should work on gently rotating the knee to the inside.

### The Lower Leg

The lower leg should hang down loosely against the horse's body. Please don't squeeze: your horse cannot move in a relaxed manner when you wrap around him like a vise. When you overuse the lower leg by pressing it against the horse, you run the risk that your knees will open, causing your upper leg to no longer lie in the correct position.

The radius of movement of the rider's lower leg on the horse is often completely exaggerated. We often see the lower leg, in jumping as well as in dressage, flying from the girth to the saddle pad. This is wrong in both disciplines. Bringing the leg far back and up is only possible when the rider moves the lower leg from the knee, but this is incorrect! The position of the lower leg should be at the girth to about a hands-breadth behind it. It is enough when I take the leg a little way back from the hip without making a huge movement of the lower leg from the knee. The lower leg should be taken a little back for some signals, for example, going into the canter,

*Wrong! The lower leg is pulled up and back from the knee causing the aid to be given in a bad spot way too far back on the horse's side.*

but not upward. Horses respond very well to a deep aid of the leg in the region of the girth, but not so well to an aid given far back and up near the saddle pad. This causes many horses to brace or wring their tail.

### The Ankle

The ankle is a very important joint for a rider. When it is stiff, it is difficult to give a fine, soft aid—it must be mobile in order to control the position of the toes and correctly use the spurs in more advanced stages. A good rider should be able to use the spurs to ruffle the horse's fur against the direction of growth and to touch the horse's body on the right place with the right intensity. This is not possible with a stiff ankle.

The ankle should not force the heel down, because a deep heel causes a hard calf muscle. Contact with a consistently hard calf is uncomfortable for the horse and can make him tense and dull. It is impossible to give fine aids with constantly tight muscles. Such attempts end up making a horse dull or causing him to push back.

The ankle should be able to spring with the movement of the horse and keep the foot in the stirrup. In a dressage seat, the foot should not press on the stirrup, but should lie in it softly. When the rider has a lot of weight on the foot in the stirrup, her weight is not on her seat, and she is standing on the horse. In this position, it is impossible to correctly aid with the seat.

### The Toes

The toes should be carried absolutely parallel to the horse's body. People often have difficulty with ankle mobility and their toes stick out. This error often goes along with knees turning out, too. Regular gymnastic exercises turning the foot outward and inward can help. When the toes turn out, the rider always allows the heel, and in the worst case, the spur, to be in constant contact with the horse's body, which quickly dulls the horse's responsiveness. Obviously, the toes should not point down either. When this happens, the rider is either pulling the legs up instead of letting them hang down, or she can't rest her foot quietly in the stirrup because it is too long. Both cases make it impossible to give precise aids.

## Harmoniously Following the Movement

### Try Not to Be Defensive and "Against" the Movement

The rider should "receive" the movement of the horse. This is easy when you are at the walk, but the transition to trot is when problems begin. Few riders are able to accept what the horse offers in movement and follow it with a mobile pelvis. Most beginners try to protect themselves against bouncing at the trot. Feigning a quiet seat, they clamp on with the legs or try to sit still—holding their breath—with a stiff pelvis, despite the lively movement of the horse. This works for only a short time before the rider is out of breath and strength, and she loses her posture. In the meantime, the horse has become extremely tense because the bouncing burden on his back bothers him and this, of course, makes it even more difficult for the rider to sit comfortably. It is a vicious cycle of poor sitting and a tense horse's back.

*Consequently, I urgently recommend to every rider to try to sit in a relaxed manner and breathe as if you were walking. Use your stomach and back muscles and hold your upper body still.*

You should accept and follow the movement of the horse with the movement of your pelvis while your arms and legs fall down loose. If you can't do this, you should find a riding instructor to give you lessons while you are being longed. Even if you have been riding for a long time, it isn't a bad thing to do, and it demonstrates that you understand the art of riding and you respect the horse.

There are also riders that try not to resist the movements of the horse and stay with the horse through exaggerated movement of their own body. This is also not correct because the horse will feel just as upset as with a stiff rider—he has to search out of the jumble of the rider's movements the one movement that is an aid and somehow ignore the rest.

### Listen to the Natural Rhythm of the Horse

This is another important point: the rider is most comfortable for the horse to carry when she can follow the horse's natural rhythm. Many riders have their own rhythm in their head and follow that one, thus overriding the horse's rhythm. The horse comes out of balance and starts running on the forehand, which makes sitting more difficult. The ride is harmonious only when the rider is able to hear the horse's natural rhythm of movement. For many riders, this requires ignoring themselves and "feeling their way into" their horse partner. This is no easy undertaking because it requires a mental willingness to do so.

*Relaxing and letting yourself into the rhythm of the horse, without always trying to force it, requires inner quiet. Anja Beran on Favory Toscana in a supple, rhythmical, posting trot.*

## Have the Courage to Do Nothing

"Feeling" riders express themselves through a certain courage to do nothing. When everything is going well and the horse is willing and light and rhythmical in the gait, the rider should now and then remove, or at least minimize, the aids to keep the horse sensitive and also to praise him. This keeps him motivated.

*The rider should use an aid only when indicated: because the exercise or the horse's carriage needs to be changed. This requires a consciousness that you are not merely engaging in a sport on a living being, but are striving for a harmonious partnership and, therefore, treating the animal with care.*

My riding is not better the more I drive, hold, and sweat. Rather, the less I agitate the horse, the higher the level of my riding, as long as I am able to allow my horse to shine full of energy. It is more aesthetic when I can influence the horse invisibly, because I want my horse to be the focus, not me.

Doing nothing allows me to be in sync with the horse's movement without worrying about constantly supporting him or wanting to change something. Let go!

*When it feels good, do nothing! Let the horse do it, smile and enjoy the moment. Vera Munderloh on the Westfalian gelding Flamingo in "descente de main" (giving the hand).*

## Give Aids Consciously

As soon as you begin the first unrestricted rides off the longe, you must give aids because you need to guide the horse—at least in direction and gait. The time for merely being a passenger and getting yourself in sync with the horse is behind you. This is the moment when many riders lose the basic seat that was carefully developed on the longe, because they think they must be constantly doing something. Excessive activity destroys a beautiful seat, especially when the first attempts at riding off the longe are on a horse that is stiff and dull to the aids. In order not to make your horse nervous with constant aids, you need to get accustomed to giving aids consciously—that is, only when they are necessary and, above all, as invisibly as possible. Naturally, you can't allow your horse to not respond—you must correct him and ask again more clearly and then immediately lighten up. Many riders make their horse dependent on big aids and forget to perfect their seat. I recommend to these riders that they stop for a moment, check their seat in the saddle, and think about losing the need for constant agitation.

## Correcting Your Seat Can Make Aids Unnecessary

In general, no aid should be given monotonously or without intention. The rider should consciously think about the aid before giving it. The seat is the basis and the prerequisite for giving clear and fine aids. In the following chapter, I will talk about making a beautiful seat into an effective seat. Just because you can follow the movement of the horse with suppleness doesn't mean you are able to aid in the right moment with the right intensity. This ability must be carefully developed, because many riders lose the elegant seat they worked so hard to develop as soon as they begin to influence the horse. This can be avoided with competent instruction. You must learn to use your body so that you give the correct signal to the horse at the right moment. You must support the horse with your body, so that he can maintain his balance. You must transition from a passive role, in which you merely follow the horse, to an active role in order to be able to ride exercises and improve him.

Influencing the horse should not be at the cost of the seat. The rider can best learn to understand this on a well-trained horse, so she can reduce the aid and learn just how little it takes of a sensitive aid for the horse to promptly respond. This gives the rider an "aha" experience, which improves the interplay of the aids. The horse shows her how.

Imagine you have carefully developed a supple seat on the longe, you can control your body well, and you are now starting to ride off the longe. Unfortunately, you are not on a well-trained school horse but on a heavy stiff horse that scarcely takes an independent step. Carefully you add leg, no reaction. You press harder—nothing. But you want to ride, so you start to rub and hit with the heel until the poor animal is tortured into moving. As soon as you reduce the pressure you feel that he will immediately slow down and stop. From now on, you don't think any more about your seat or your posture. Everything that you do in the saddle is focused on the effort of driving the horse forward. Gradually, you start raising your legs, pressing and squeezing as much as possible in order to keep the horse going. Your seat will suffer under this effort and it is impossible to develop a feeling for a sensitive aid. That is an example of how a rider can be ruined by a poorly trained horse, and shows the critical role of a school horse.

*Give slightly and move freshly forward! Briefly softening the contact checks for self-carriage. Vera Munderloh on Ciclone.*

# ADVANCED CONCEPTS

## FROM A SUPPLE SEAT TO AIDING EFFECTIVELY

*"As soon as the rider has learned to use her body to advantage, she will follow the laws of the riding art with the proper position of her limbs and be able to perform the fine movements in this art after many years of effort. The position of the limbs determines how you can use their strength."* –Dupaty de Clam

Die Reitkunst im Spiegel ihrer Meister (The art of riding as seen through its masters) by Bertold Schirg (Olms Verlag, 1987)

There is no one correct seat. The seat is dependent on the age and level of training of the horse and also on the situation at the moment. I can't sit as heavily on a young horse as on a trained horse, and I can't sit on a horse in the process of being reschooled as I can on a solid, educated horse. Likewise, there are special situations that require an appropriate seat, for example, when a horse suddenly bolts.

The seat is also not static and mechanical, but is dynamic and must be very flexible. There are riders who understand this and can ride all kinds of horses well. Others find the need to adjust their seat very difficult, and they can only attain a specific level on certain horses.

I have often seen riders that sit very elegantly on a horse, but unfortunately, have not been taught well enough about how to effectively use their seat. Others sit less correctly or aesthetically, but can very sensitively adjust to the horse's movements. They know how to use their body to positively influence the horse, which saves them a lot of hand and leg use. You can most accurately read the quality of the seat in the horse himself: Does he move in all three gaits correctly, especially at the walk? Is he collected? Is he happy to move and expressive? Does he have a quiet head-neck carriage? If you are still unsure about this, you can examine the horse without a saddle. A strong back that is well muscled and not sore says a lot about the rider's seat.

## The Seat as a Means of Communication

The rider gives the aids from the seat. The aids should form a clear and intentional language to communicate with the horse but the aids can only be clear when the rider is able to give them exactly when needed. This requires perfect body control and coordination in the rider. You have to have your own body well under control to be able to control a 1200-pound foreign body. This is where many riders fail: they want to influence the horse, but lack the coordination to give the aids clearly.

*The horse is then in the difficult position of filtering out the signals that have meaning from the mix of intentional and miscellaneous movements of the rider. Not so easy to do!*

As a result, many horses become resigned and dull. Their motivation sinks and the rider has to give a very clear aid to get a reaction at all. Others get nervous because they don't know how to react to whatever it is the rider might want, because the rider is always sending contradictory signals. These horses become tense and difficult. Unfortunately, these horses also typically get labeled as unrideable only because they feel overwhelmed by the disturbing burden on their back. Their lives usually end in a sad situation. Simple responsibility and respect for the creature should be enough to get us to continually work on our seat and our body control.

*A supple, controlled seat is the basis for communicating fine aids to the horse.*

*Forward with swing. Not just from the legs, but more from the seat. Anja Beran on Favory Toscana.*

## The Seat at the Walk

The walk is the easiest gait for riders to sit quietly in the saddle because there is no impulsion. Later, at advanced levels, many students have the most trouble with the walk. This is because the walk is no longer carefully ridden today. It is merely practiced with long reins to warm up the horse before working, and later, to take a break.

The problems start when the rider takes up the reins to *really* ride the walk. Most riders don't have the inner calmness to "melt" into the horse and do little in this slow gait with no impulsion. They want to "do stuff" from the saddle. This is seen in a constant harassment of the horse with legs, hands, seat, and upper body that are constantly moving. It is easy to understand that the horse can't relax with gymnastics happening on his back. A rider that continually pushes disturbs the horse's back so much that muscular problems can develop. Constant driving can also cause the horse to move past his tempo, while a closed hand contradicts the leg aid. The result is horses that are locked up at the walk, move on the forehand, and finally, start pacing.

*The most important commandment at the walk is to listen to the horse and to orient yourself to his individual stride.*

You should be erect and the spine should be lengthened. Only the pelvis follows the movement, while the rest of the upper body is held as still as possible. When you make yourself tall, the horse is in the position to elevate himself. How can a rider that is slouching without any posture or muscle tension expect her horse to lift? When your upper body is erect, the back and abdominal muscles provide stability. It is also important to let your arms and legs hang loose so that you can give sensitive impulses with

The Spanish walk teaches the rider to sit with erect posture and positive tension even at a walk that lacks impulsion. Vera Munderloh on the P.R.E. stallion Alaraz.

the leg or the fingers. In this way, you can straighten and collect the horse. Understandably, the pelvis of the rider moves less at the collected walk than in the extended walk. For the latter, the rider must open the fingers so that the horse can lengthen his neck and transition from a carrying hind leg to a pushing hind leg. The horse also lengthens his frame. To bring him back to a collected walk, merely follow the big walk movement less with the pelvis. The horse can feel that the rider isn't "walking" with him anymore and will immediately shorten the length of his step. At the same time, the rider pulls herself up straighter and, if necessary, turns the hand a little inward in order to bring the horse back. A well-trained horse will immediately collect and elevate, and transition from pushing to carrying.

We have different types of walk to sit to, according to tempo and degree of collection. Patient and detailed experimentation with the influences of the seat at the calm gait of walk is terribly ignored today. I can only fervently urge every rider to test daily how you can use your body to get different responses from the horse. The horse's movement at the walk affects (disturbs) our seat the least. Consequently, you can use your body in a very precise and sensitive way and, for example, try to perform the lateral movements in a walk, or transition into halt and rein-back followed by moving forward at the walk with everything being as soft, slow, and supple as possible with almost no use of the hand at all. Try hanging your hands loosely and apathetically and don't move your relaxed arms at all. Try to get the feeling that you can control each leg of the horse—how quickly it moves and to where. You will be surprised to see what fine nuances of body movement you can use to achieve a whispering communication: a hint of moving forward with your upper body or a tiny straightening will cause a reaction in your horse just as a slight turn of the upper body.

Convince yourself! Test your seat in the smallest detail and observe your horse closely. The horse will become more interested and sensitive with this work. He will listen intently to correctly interpret your soft indication, because he wants to please you and will be highly motivated to try to follow your body language.

*"Try to awaken curiosity with the lightness of your aids."* —Nuno Oliveira

Notizen zum Unterricht (Teaching notes) by Nuno Oliveira (Olms Verlag, 1998)

Imagine that you move on the horse only as much as necessary so someone watching won't be able to tell what you want the horse to do, and won't understand why your horse is doing this or that because he can't see any aids. I always tell my riding students with a wink that they should give the aids as invisibly as possible so that no one knows what they are going to ride next. If it doesn't happen, it isn't so upsetting! Seriously, imagine you pull your outside leg exaggeratedly back and up and give a distinctly visible spur to make the horse canter and—nothing happens. This is ugly and embarrassing. When something goes wrong, it is enough for you and your horse to know it and not all the spectators. For this reason alone, you should strive for as light an aid as possible.

As soon as you have reached the stage at the walk where you sit on a softly chewing, supple horse that is independent of the hand and dependent on the seat, you should try to apply what you have learned to the trot.

This is not so easy since your body goes easily out of control at the trot, because you now have *Schwung* (swing) and bounce. It is hard to aid as precisely at the trot as at the walk. Nevertheless, it is important for you to see what you can do at the trot with the magic you experienced at the walk when controlling the horse's huge body with the minimal aids of your seat. Just because the trot is faster and more powerful, your aids must not become stronger or less precise. The aesthetics lie in the invisibility. Always bear in mind that you want your horse on display, not yourself. Your inner self influences your seat. Are you calm, patient, with humble restraint and sensitivity coupled with energy, effort, and a proud posture so you can sit as you strive to? Your physical capabilities are involved. Do you have the strength, coordination, and relaxation necessary to use your body as you want? And can you still breathe easily with all of this concentration? Check your facial expressions. Many riders grimace when riding. Make your face soft!

You can see how complex the whole business is. If you are missing one building block, the whole system suffers for it. This is why we never learn to ride perfectly because it is a huge development process that continues for the rest of our lives. Certainly the level of riding changes, but learning always continues, regardless of what level we have achieved.

In the next section, we will try to achieve a supple seat at the trot so that we can develop sensitivity in giving the aids at this gait.

*If you can truly ride a collected walk from the seat, the transition to the piaffe is very easy. Anja Beran on Favory Toscana.*

## The Seat at the Trot

Before I talk about the sitting trot, I would like to discuss the posting trot. There are some details about this way of riding the trot that are especially important for young horses and are crucial for the well-being and unfettered movement of the horse.

First, you need an appropriate grip with the knee, because you lift yourself from the knee. You don't stand up from the stirrup. Your lower leg and the stirrup should stay stable and still. Your hands and arms remain independent and are not involved in the up and down of the posting trot, but remain still and down. This requires the elbows to open and close with the post. For people that have a problem with this, I recommend they put their hands left and right in front of the saddle on the horse's neck, and keep them in this position while posting the trot. In this way, the hand is quiet, the contact is even, and the rider can concentrate on standing up and sitting down in the saddle. When standing up, you should try to think diagonally forward and up instead of standing up vertically. This is necessary because you are in a dynamic process and the horse is moving forward under you. If you take your upper body a little forward it will help you not to get behind the movement, especially if your horse makes an unexpected jump forward.

You should stand up when the horse's outside shoulder goes forward. Sitting back down in the saddle requires muscle and positive tension. Come into the saddle slowly

*A harmonious posting trot with soft contact: Anja Beran on the young P.R.E. stallion Nadal.*

and carefully. Don't just fall down weakly. You should also try to touch the saddle at the deepest point without hitting your seat against the cantle. When you have found the right rhythm and follow these points, the horse will relax as he trots forward. There is harmony between both bodies.

When you trot off, stay sitting for the first two or three steps and then start posting. If you try to stand right with the first trot step, it will be harder to find the rhythm, it looks clumsy, and most of all, you disturb the horse.

## The Sitting Trot

In order to transition from a walk to a trot that you can sit well, the walk needs to be as collected as possible and the horse must move in balance. From this expressive walk that is naturally very light in the hand, give a polite but not sudden command with the leg and let him trot. While you give this aid, bring your navel slightly forward in the direction of your hands and while relaxed, wait for the first trot step. Now follow the movement that the horse presents you. In no way should you brace against the movement with legs clamped on. If you try to do that, you will cramp and limit your breathing, and going along in sync with the movement will be impossible. Your tension will carry over to the horse very quickly and you will no longer be allowed to sit while relaxed because he will lock up his back. If you feel this happening, ask a competent person to put you on the longe. Practice sitting the trot with instruction until you feel comfortable and can follow the movement in relaxation. Also, make sure your breathing is relaxed. This small step back to the longe line will quickly give you a huge step forward in riding and should absolutely be done.

The second big mistake that often happens is when the rider can't get into the

*An extended trot requires body strength, and the hand must move softly forward to allow the frame to lengthen. Vera Munderloh on Novilunio.*

rhythm of the horse, even though she might not have a problem sitting the movement. Furthermore, she might try to keep the horse going by constantly pushing with her seat. She doesn't realize that with all this activity she is disturbing the horse greatly in his back, which eventually makes him more and more lazy and slow. She has the impression that everything is in movement and she has to constantly work to keep it that way. At the end of the riding lesson, she thinks she has worked hard and that everything ought to be good. Since the horse also had to work hard,

the lesson is considered positive. These riders are hard to correct, because it is difficult for them to "let go" and allow themselves to "get into the horse."

In this case, correcting the seat begins with the head: the rider must try to change her attitude, slow down a little, and relax. Instruction on the longe is useful here as well, but not to improve the seat so much as to teach the rider that she doesn't need to be constantly doing something. She must learn the courage of passivity. A video of her riding can be very helpful. She probably doesn't

realize how active she is on the horse and how unattractive it looks. The concepts that lead to a better seat in this case are better body awareness, inner calm, and also more understanding and feeling for the horse.

But now back to our correct transition into trot with the navel slightly forward and the pelvis receiving the first trot steps. Follow the movement with a mobile pelvis and a stable stomach and back musculature that doesn't let you collapse, but rather helps you keep the upper body straight, meaning erect and stable. Breathe evenly, deeply, and

*Maintain good posture while still following the movement with suppleness. Only in this way can the horse develop optimally. Anja Beran on the Lusitano stallion Campeao.*

the beginning, this analysis takes a while during which time the horse is not moving ideally. However, the rider will gain experience, patience, and such a regimen that she gradually learns to know ahead of time what her horse is going to do in the next few feet. Then she can quietly, preventively influence the horse so that a spectator can't see her doing it—only seeing a horse/rider pair in harmony.

A more beautiful and effective seat comes from understanding the horse as well as from excellent body control. It isn't enough to have one of the two. Constantly listening to the horse is just as important as adjusting to following the lines. Every corner, every circle requires an adjustment of the seat. The rider can't remain static but must be flexible as she follows the horse. Even while trotting, she should turn with the horse on a curved line and try to adjust her shoulders to those of her horse, while keeping the shoulders above the pelvis. It takes a long time to learn these complex movements in the saddle, and requires many years of practice and thinking about it.

A big mistake that is often made on horses that are a little uncomfortable is to lean back with the upper body so that the pelvis can better follow the movement. This actually works because the pelvis can more easily get into the movement of the horse in this position, but correct aids are no longer possible and the rider is sitting heavily behind the center of gravity.

Keep checking in the arena mirrors that you are erect and not "lying" behind the vertical. In your house, stand sideways in front of a mirror and check whether you have the correct perception of erect posture. Bend your knees a little, with the feet a hip's breadth apart and see if your upper body is vertical or if you are leaning back or forward. In general, leaning backward is more common.

calmly. Most seat problems begin when the rider starts giving aids. Try to govern this by first analyzing what exactly is happening beneath you. Do you feel, for example, that your horse is losing energy? If so, give a polite, invisible leg aid to keep him going. The driving aid always comes from the leg and not from an exaggerated pushing pelvis or upper body. If your horse doesn't respond, give another stronger leg aid with a tap of the whip. Remember to give a little forward with your hands when you use these driving aids to make the way forward easier to

find. If your horse responds well, don't forget to praise him and return to your relaxed seat until the moment when it is necessary to influence him again. The rider that can analyze what the horse is doing now and what aid she should give—and can do that clearly—will ride her horse with sensitivity and be able to sit well.

Riders who constantly give random aids of arbitrary intensity should think about the logic of doing that. They will dull their horse over time and make him tense in the back, which makes sitting more difficult. In

*Even when there is a great deal of impulsion, go with the horse instead of hindering him. Anja Beran on Favory Toscana.*

Many riders fall forward onto their thighs and press the seat toward the saddle cantle when the horse's trot is uncomfortable for them. The lower back hollows in this position, the pelvis is locked, and it is impossible to follow the movement with suppleness. The horse will quickly react to you sitting this way by stiffening, which makes the correct seat even more difficult.

A supple seat and a relaxed horse's back that invites the rider to sit are inter-dependent.

Otherwise you have a vicious cycle: the rider doesn't sit well, and the horse defends himself by tightening his back, which causes the rider not to be able to sit any more.

When you are trotting in harmony with your horse, don't forget to check your seat frequently with a check list: Am I sitting straight? Are my arms falling loosely down? What are my wrists doing? Are my feet resting in the stirrups? Is my leg relaxed? Am I looking forward? Question after question must be checked rou-

tinely. Anyone who rides without an instructor must check herself as best she can.

*It is impossible to influence a 1,100 pound horse's body without coordinating your own body.*

After focusing for a moment on your own body at the trot, you must concentrate again on your horse: Is he in balance and is there enough *Schwung* (swing)? What should you

*Soften the posture a little and let the horse relax.*

do next in order to make him pay attention or to activate him more? As soon as you have decided that, you have to choose the appropriate aids, which are never in isolation, but must be given together with the seat. For example, if you want to go into a shoulder-in coming out of a corner, it is not enough to steer the horse with the reins and legs into the movement, which is seen all too often. More importantly, you must take your weight a little in the direction of the movement and,

above all, turn your upper body and pelvis, just as if you were going to ride across the diagonal after the corner.

This interplay of seat, a slight shift of weight, and turning of the upper body make for fine riding, and at the same time, minimizes the use of the rein and leg aids. Riding becomes body language. Hands and legs become useful accessories that no longer play a main role. This goes for riding any gait and in all movements. The rider that doesn't

know how to correctly use her body as an aid has to use the hands and legs more. This is because she is contradicting the other aids with how she uses her body. She must often give rough aids, because otherwise the horse doesn't understand. The seat tells the horse: Do this! And the hands and legs say: Do that! This confuses the animal and he will ultimately follow the aid that is the strongest. It doesn't need to be said that this robs the horse of all motivation.

*Don't push with your seat. Just softly receive the canter stride.*

## The Seat at the Canter

Many unfortunate sayings like "wipe the sad-dle" or "push the horse forward" lead to quite an undesirable scene when you watch riders cantering. As an observer, you quickly get the impression that this gait requires a lot of sweating, and that the rider must work hard and use a lot of energy and strength. It would be so lovely if she would just let the horse canter and go along with him instead of bother-ing him. In order to do this, the rider should imagine that she receives and follows every canter stride. This means she shouldn't make any movements on her own, just merely go along with what the horse gives her.

The rider should never push hard with her seat because the swing that naturally occurs at the canter only once in the stride increases the effect of this pushing, causing a huge disturbance on the horse's back: he tenses his back muscles and is unwilling to canter forward.

*Go unobtrusively with the horse and make him the center of attention.*

The uneducated rider responds by pushing more and the vicious cycle begins. It is better to imagine that you sit completely still and accompany your horse with the pelvis as the upper body stays as quiet as possible. Every driving impulse forward should come from your inside leg and not with a huge swing of the upper body. The outside leg gives the start signal for the canter. Why? Because the outside hind leg is the first step of the canter stride. After that, the inside leg takes over the command for going forward, as is necessary. You must be conscious of this and free yourself from any intention to push forcefully with your body.

"Wiping the saddle" with the seat not only looks unaesthetic, it also hinders the rider from sitting quietly in the deepest part of the saddle. A saddle is not a slide. It is a place to sit with respect and in balance, because you are sitting on the sensitive back of a living creature.

*Shoulders and arms fall down relaxed, the upper body is stable, and the rider looks forward between the ears of the horse. Vera Munderloh on the Lusitano stallion Vinho.*

In order to make the horse "sit" more at the canter, the rider is not limited to taking with the hands and activating with the leg. She can use her seat by not following the canter so strongly. The horse feels that she is not going harmoniously with him anymore and will adjust himself to her seat by shortening his canter stride. In this way, he comes back in sync with his rider. Practically speaking, the rider needs strong stomach and back muscles and must imagine that she pulls herself up higher and hesitates for a moment if she wants to keep her upper body more on the spot, instead of going freely forward with the horse. Bringing the horse up from the seat is best practiced on a well-trained

horse. Once you have felt how to use your seat in this way—and can do it—you won't have to use the other aids as much. The canter becomes expressive and no one can see how the rider is guiding her horse because she can shrink the aids to a minimum.

*The better the seat, the more the horse can be ridden independently of the reins, and the more motivated most horses become.*

When speeding up the canter, take the upper body slightly forward, add the leg aid, and open the fingers to make going more forward easier. During the increase in speed, follow the horse in the usual way. If

you want to speed up again, repeat the process or straighten yourself up, and continue as described above to bring the horse back under you with as little use of the hand as possible.

*To extend the canter with impulsion, the rider's hand and upper body move slightly forward. Vera Munderloh on the Lusitano stallion Super.*

*A transition from piaffe to passage. The sternum is pushed slightly forward, the hand goes slightly forward and downward, while the legs lightly activate. Vera Munderloh on Vinho.*

## Riding Transitions

To ride a transition, you must interrupt the harmonious flow of movement. You don't want to merely ride with a hand and leg effect: to make more use of your seat, you need to use it to interrupt the flow. How do you do this? Imagine you are trotting along and would like to break to a walk. Your pelvis follows the rhythm of the horse with suppleness, and arms and shoulders hang down loosely with softly closed fists. Your upper body has positive tension while your legs hang down loose in light contact with the horse's body, ready to be used. This position of the pelvis and the leg is an important prerequisite for being able to ride a transition from the seat.

If you suddenly don't follow with suppleness, you are disturbing the horse in the back and he will promptly react and interrupt his movement, just as you have interrupted yours. You must try to stop your pelvis from swinging with the horse for a few seconds.

*Transition from the piaffe to the passage on a volte: Anja Beran on the P.R.E. stallion Ofendido.*

To do this, briefly close the knee and thigh to stabilize the pelvis. As soon as you feel that your horse is stopping, let your legs hang loosely again. If the horse doesn't respond as you want, it doesn't help to keep on squeezing. You must repeat the process until you have a positive reaction and then immediately praise him. Horses whose riders constantly squeeze with the leg don't respond to this aid any more, even if they are supposed to be going forward. Horses also won't react as desired if their riders never swing the pelvis with the horse but sit stiffly, thus restricting the horse's flow of movement in his back. Horses that have been dulled and ruined by poor riders need a corrective ride in order to make them loose again and to sensitize them to fine aids. We often hear that a horse is lazy. In this case, the seat of the rider must be checked, because when it blocks the horse, he tenses his musculature and can't go forward comfortably anymore.

A transition with fine aids from a correct seat is completely possible, but the rider must be able to coordinate her body well. The interplay between opening and closing the legs, and tensing and relaxing the musculature, must be controlled down to the smallest detail if you are going to influence a powerful horse without rough aids.

Other transitions, whether from walk to halt, trot to halt, or canter to walk are ridden the same way. If the aid from the seat isn't enough, the outside rein can support the transition while the inside rein holds the flexion. It also helps to accompany the down transition with a deep exhale.

There is a common mistake that occurs in the transition to walk. Many riders transition correctly, but don't maintain their body tension after the transition and collapse. This causes the horse to fall apart and go on the forehand. The rider feels this and tries to correct the problem with more driving, which leads to the horse running on the forehand. Consequently, it is very important to keep sitting quietly, erect, and with positive tension in the upper body after the transition to walk, so that the horse stays on the aids and in good carriage, instead of pushing him on the forehand. Only in this way can he maintain his balance and be ready for the next action.

*In order to perfect the feeling for transitions, the rider most of all needs an excellently trained horse. The oft-repeated explanations of the riding instructor won't lead to success when the horse can't give the rider an "aha" experience.*

## The Rein-Back

A common mistake seen in the rein-back is to lean forward, holding the reins short, and pulling both lower legs back and up. Because the rider is lying on the forehand, the horse is very short in the neck and drags backward with stiff legs behind, leaving a trail in the footing of the arena. Leaning forward with the upper body causes the horse to get long in the back so that the hind legs stick out behind instead of staying underneath. This results in the horse creeping backward. Moving backward in this way is not just physically uncomfortable for the horse, it is also illogical, which makes it hard to follow the aids. Why?

When a rider wants to ride off like a jockey on a racehorse out of a starting gate, or when she wants to speed up the gait, she will logically lean forward, first of all to not get behind the movement of the horse, and secondly, to free up the horse's back to make a prompt move-off easier.

*Remember: when the upper body is forward, your back is slightly unloaded, which signals the horse to move forward.*

If you want to collect a horse to slow him in the gait, like getting the canter to "sit" more, you straighten yourself up more and take your weight a tiny bit backward. Your horse will immediately lift up, stride more actively, and collect more. So, straightening up the upper body and loading the horse's back a little more signals the horse to collect.

Why do you do exactly the opposite in the rein-back? Many instructors say it is to unload the horse's back. I don't share this opinion because it is not necessary. When a horse is correctly trained from the beginning, he can easily do this exercise with a rider that sits well. You don't want to pull the horse back: he should step back willingly and in collection, in sync with your body.

It makes more sense, therefore, to straighten up, take your shoulders slightly back while your legs stay in place, or aid a little at the girth. In earlier times, a rider would back her horse by taking her shoulders back and using the spurs at the girth. This kept the hands free for other actions that were more important than just using the reins.

When you raise yourself up more, your horse also raises up, and when you sit more into him, he will sink his haunches a little and willingly step back. You should close your fingers on the reins a little at the beginning to make it clear to the horse that his energy must now flow backward in the direction indicated by your weight and upper body. With these aids, he grows "higher" in front, which is not the same as the horse going above the bit: he lowers his hind end and gets "shorter" behind. He is collected! By using the seat correctly in the rein-back, you can collect the horse. Instead of getting long and deep and on the forehand, he can benefit from this exercise: when correctly done, the rein-back has high gymnastic value. This puts the horse in the position to start the piaffe, start a collected canter, or do whatever you want because the forehand is now maximally unloaded.

*Whether or not a horse benefits from a movement doesn't depend on how many times you repeat it. Most important is how you are sitting in the exercise.*

Sitting, as just described, helps your horse to stay motivated and sharp. You are communicating in a clear and logical way with him instead of requiring that one time he goes forward when you take your upper body forward, and another time, he should suddenly go backward.

## The Seat in the Lateral Movements

A horse that is moving sideways offers many challenges for the rider's seat. The attempt to follow lateral movements with suppleness very often fails due to the rider's lack of body awareness.

### The Leg-Yield

I will begin with the simplest initial sideways steps of the horse, the leg-yield. It doesn't matter if you are practicing at the walk or the trot. Assume you are traveling to the left and want to do a right leg-yield along the long side. How should you use your body to achieve the movement?

First, flex your horse a slight bit to the outside right before the second corner of the short side, and cut off the corner by riding at an angle to the wall. I turn my upper body and pelvis toward the wall. Pay attention because, at this moment, the following almost always happens:

- One shoulder goes higher or lower than the other.

- Your shoulders turn toward the wall but your pelvis is locked up and doesn't come along.

- Your waist collapses with the attempt to turn your body.

- Your weight goes completely to one side of the saddle when you just simply want to turn your body.

- Your outside leg sticks out stiffly while the inside leg is pulled up and clamps on.

Pay strict attention to turning the upper body in one block so that your shoulders stay parallel with, and exactly over, the hips. Check yourself in a mirror that is placed on the long side of the arena or have yourself videotaped, especially from behind. Be conscious of the position of your legs and try to load the seat bone a little more in the direction you are riding. Being constantly aware of all your body parts is endlessly important for riding and requires frequently asking yourself about your position. Often, quietly go through a checklist about your body. You will need to check the problem areas that you know about. Gradually, you will develop a better feel for erect posture with the right level of body tension. It is always easier to give the desired aids correctly and to make adjustments as needed out of a correct position.

When you have achieved this stage of body awareness with the necessary coordination and mobility, you can consider shaping the horse. Any attempts to train a horse or to improve a horse in some way before you have reached this state will fail, or lead to results that aren't consistent with the ideals of a classically ridden horse but rather a robotic creature that is far from "through" and balanced. The seat is always the key to success. I can promise you that regardless of the level of riding, you will never stop trying to improve your seat.

### The Shoulder-In

The next lateral movement is the shoulder-in. After riding deep through a corner turn on the diagonal. It helps if you take your eyes along in the turn and look at the diagonal.

*The upper body is turned slightly toward the inside of the arena, and the shoulders are aligned with the horse's shoulders. Katharina Reinthaler on the Frederiksborger stallion Sirius in shoulder-in at the trot.*

*Shoulder-in on the circle. The inside rein is pushed slightly forward to check that the horse is truly on the aids rather than being held in the bend and flexion. The rider sits deep but relaxed on the horse. Vera Munderloh on Super.*

You differentiate between the closed hand and the opening hand. In the shoulder-in the closed hand is usually on the outside. The outside rein presses softly against the neck and encourages the horse's shoulders to the inside. The exercise actually should be called "shoulders-in." The opening inside hand moves slightly to the side, helps to maintain flexion, and also supports the inside leg, making it easier for the horse to step sideways. The outside rein is taken up as necessary, for example, when the horse wants to continue down the diagonal once he has brought his forehand toward the inside. The outside rein prevents this and assures that the horse stays in the shoulder-in while the hindquarters continue down the track. The inside leg drives sideways and the outside leg prevents the shoulders from escaping, and also prevents the hindquarters from evading sideways toward the rail.

Ideally, you should imagine that your seat leads the horse into the shoulder-in, in that you guide the forehand inward and then the outside rein catches the horse while your inside leg drives softly sideways. Under no circumstances should you think about pushing the hindquarters to the side. That would be backward. Above all, you must be sure that you are speaking clearly to the horse so that he doesn't misunderstand, and that you sit in the direction of the movement. This means sitting to the outside in the shoulder-in. In this way, the horse learns from the beginning to always follow your weight, and you can use this subtle hint from your seat constantly without an observer noticing it.

## The Travers and Renvers

In travers, you turn toward the rail, analogous to the leg-yield. But now your horse is bent and flexed in the direction of travel. You use your inside leg at the girth and imagine that the horse wraps around it. This is decisive for the bend. The inside hand helps to get bend and flexion and softens as soon as the horse has responded. If the horse loses bend or flexion, the inside hand helps to get it back again. The outside hand holds the contact and leads the forehand a little sideways by pressing the rein lightly against the neck. The outside hand can also be moved outward when the hindquarters don't move sideways enough. The outside leg brings the croup around and softens immediately when the horse goes sideways. You sit in the direction of the movement. Stepping on the stirrup is a good way to use the weight aid. This means that you step a little harder on the inside stirrup, which brings your weight a little more to this side. The sensitively ridden horse will immediately understand which way he is supposed to move. It is very important for this—and all lateral movements—to keep your weight constantly on this side.

*Travers to the left, ridden with an erect posture, correct turn of the body, and very relaxed arms. Anja Beran on Ofendido.*

*Renvers with swing and lightness in the hand. Anja Beran on the Lusitano stallion Regedor.*

*Renvers with very good bend. The rider's shoulders are exactly aligned with the horse's shoulders. Anja Beran on Ofendido.*

*Travers being ridden at the canter and on the circle. It is important for a sensitive seat and hand to allow the horse to elevate and "blossom."*

Many riders tend to "waddle" (like a duck) left and right in the saddle in the belief that they are helping the lateral movement. The opposite is true. The horse becomes insecure and unstable due to this "waddling." He isn't sure he should stay in the lateral movement anymore, because the seat signals something else than what the hand and leg aids are saying. The horse hears from the seat that he should change direction while the reins and legs tell him to go in the same direction. Yes, you guessed it: the horse will get frustrated and become dull to the weight aid. Your uncoordinated body contradicts your other aids and, as a result, your horse doesn't understand anymore and he loses motivation.

You sit the same in the renvers as in the travers, but now the hindquarters stay on the track and the forehand is brought to the inside while your horse is bent and flexed in the direction of travel. Renvers is merely the counter-movement to travers.

*As it should be! Shoulders precisely over the pelvis, lightly stepping in the left stirrup with soft contact. Silvia Wimmer on the Lusitano stallion Quilate.*

*Erect upper body with positive body tension in sync with the lateral movement of the horse. Vera Munderloh on the Lusitano stallion Novilunio.*

## The Half-Pass

When you ride a corner well and can thoughtfully bring the horse into a shoulder-fore, you can weight the stirrup at the beginning of the half-pass. My horses know immediately that when I step on the inside stirrup after a corner, which puts my weight slightly to the inside, they should go sideways on the diagonal. Ideally, you hold your shoulders exactly

*When body language works, everything looks easy. Hands and legs become accessories. Anja Beran on Ofendido.*

over the horse's shoulders and above your pelvis. Neither shoulder should be higher or lower than the other. When the horse doesn't lead well with the forehand, you can take your outside shoulder slightly forward to help the forehand to lead. If a horse has a hard time taking the hindquarters sideways, it is legitimate to take the outside shoulder back a little, which influences the hindquarters to step more sideways.

Let the arms fall down loosely and try to keep the inside hand close to the horse's neck. You relax this hand as soon as the horse is bending well and is flexed. The outside hand stays constantly in contact and can be lifted a little if the horse has the tendency to get too deep. Or, the outside hand can be

taken a little to the outside to align the horse and make him move sideways better.

You must make such decisions promptly and correctly if the half-pass is to be successful. Your body must obey you, which means you must be able to use each hand, at any second, precisely as necessary. Avoid collapsing the upper body or leaning back. You should be looking straight through the horse's ears toward the short side.

The inside leg should be at the girth. This is very important in the half-pass because the horse bends around it. Consequently, it must not be pulled away from the horse. A slight turn of the toes to the outside can help to have more feeling with the horse's body and improve the bend. The inside leg also takes the horse forward. The outside leg is taken back slightly and initiates the half-pass. But pay attention! Often the rider bends the knee and takes the leg up and back, which causes it to act on the horse much too high up toward the saddle pad.

The same error occurs when initiating the canter. This is a big mistake. It not only looks unattractive, it is also uncomfortable for the horse. Many horses respond to this leg position by swatting their tail. It is correct to take the leg a couple of inches back, but only from your hip. In this way, the leg stays long. Imagine that you want to touch the horse's body as low down as possible. If you are wearing spurs, you are able to lift the abdomen up a little. If you are careful not to commit the gross error of over-bending the leg and taking it too far back, the horse responds much better when the spur is used at the correct place way down on the body rather than near the saddle blanket. But once again, you must first be conscious of what your leg is actually doing. Does it move too little or too much? Does it stay long and deep, or does it shove back and up? Advice from a good instructor is very important.

Your saddle can also hinder you from correctly using the leg. When it is too small with large knee rolls, it fixes your leg making it difficult to move the legs and the hips without force, because they are blocked by the small seat. If you want to be a little flexible in the leg, you can only move it by bending the knee. Consequently, such saddles are inappropriate and lead to an incorrect seat; over time they can injure the rider. This clamped seat also affects the horse's back negatively in terms of mobility and relaxation. If you don't feel comfortable or secure in a saddle that offers the necessary freedom of movement, you shouldn't invest in a saddle with big knee blocks, but rather in longe lessons to better train your seat. As Gustav Steinbrecht said, the seat should not be characterized by a tight grip but by balance. This is the only thing that can give the rider security on the horse's back.

## Stepping Over

Stepping over is a lateral movement that causes many errors of the seat. Since it is practiced on a circle, it is helpful to imagine a fixed point in the center of the volte or the circle. You can use a chair or a pylon because you always want to keep the same distance from the center. This helps you get the correct bend. You turn your eyes and upper body toward this object, which results in a distinct seat aid for stepping over. The inside leg drives sideways while the outside leg and rein catch the movement and stop it at any time.

Many riders make a critical mistake as they turn their upper body. They extend the outside elbow and carry the outside hand forward while the inside hand stays back. This looks like the rider's hands are on the handlebars of a bicycle that she is riding on a curve. What is right on a bicycle is backward on a horse because the outside rein helps you turn by pressing lightly on the horse's shoulders. If you yield this rein, you lose the outside support and your horse falls over the outside shoulder. With this incorrect hand and arm position, the inside rein alone does the turning, which results in pulling the neck in and the bit sideways through the mouth. Correct turning is impossible.

The outside rein must maintain a soft contact in all lateral movements and turns while the inside rein should soften when you have the right bend and flexion. The inside hand should move forward toward the horse's mouth while the outside hand stays in place. The outside elbow should also stay in place. You can see how it is precisely the opposite on a horse as on a bicycle.

## Summary of the Seat in Lateral Movements

- Turn the entire upper body without collapsing at the waist.

- Shoulders stay at the same height and over the hips.

- Always take the weight slightly in the direction of movement.

- The outside rein maintains contact and the inside rein should soften.

- No "waddling" as the horse moves sideways.

- Let the legs be long and take the appropriate leg back a little from the hip, never from the knee.

*Maintaining upright posture without collapsing is critical in lateral movements. Anja Beran on Campeao.*

## The Seat in Canter Changes of Lead

You should always, if possible, learn flying changes on a very good school horse because they require a certain knack, since to get the change, there is a distinct use of your body combined with a precise leg aid.

Lightening your seat frees up the horse's back and makes it easier for many horses. Gradually, the aids can be refined. The better the horse understands the job, the more subtly the rider can ask for the change. Although it is a big challenge, don't miss going back and reducing the aids that must be very clear at the beginning. You are lucky when you get to train on a horse that already does the flying changes well. When learning how to use your seat in the changes, make sure, above all, that the reins are even and that the horse's neck is straight. Changing the flexion in advance of, or during, the change is not logical. You must stay sitting straight and upright with good body core tension, and carefully ask the horse for the change with the new outside leg. If you want to change to the left lead, move the left hip a little forward during the process. This causes your right shoulder to come back a little, which supports the right leg for the change.

You should simply sit quietly and wait for the flying change and go with it. Staying quietly in the saddle is easy to say and hard to do. For this reason, it is important to practice under the eyes of an experienced rider. Leaning forward and looking at the horse's shoulder are common reflexes of the rider, which must be corrected gradually. It is absolutely taboo to throw yourself around on the trained horse, because it creates anxiety when following a line and ends up with a horse swaying in the exercise.

When riding tempi changes, try to sit as quietly and centered as possible and keep your hands still. There must be equal contact on the left and right reins. According to the needs of the horse, you can carry your hands a little deeper or a little higher. Ask for the change only with the leg and follow it with your hip. To avoid the extremely ugly and illogical "swinging" leg alternating back and forth, take both legs back a little at the beginning of the tempi changes and leave them there. Then you can simply aid the change with the new outside leg. In addition, this is the only way to ride the single tempis on a small horse that has by nature very short canter strides. There is absolutely no time for a customary movement of the leg forward and backward; the aid would always be too late. The ground-covering stride of large Warmbloods allows for such leg acrobatics, but it is still neither aesthetic nor efficient. Strive from the beginning to use fine and invisible aids.

## The Seat in the Piaffe

This is the best movement for teaching a young rider to feel a correct seat. During the piaffe, the horse's back is lifted and powerful, upon which she learns to move with suppleness up and down with the back. These are ideal conditions for the rider to sit, relaxed on the horse's back.

*In a good piaffe, the horse elevates and carries himself while he steps proudly and full of energy. This is the best way for the rider to feel what lightness and balance mean. This gives her the idea of how it feels to "melt" into the horse, and she will look for this harmony in other movements. The most impactful experience a young rider can have is to piaffe on a well-trained horse. This is very important for her equestrian development.*

It is, therefore, surprising that we see so many riders today who sit poorly in the piaffe. They often lean too far forward or back with the upper body, hold the reins very short in a high and tight fist, nod the head in the rhythm, and bend the lower leg too much at the knee, which puts the lower leg up and back so that the spur is near the saddle pad. The horse presents himself equally poorly: no energy, often uneven in the step, too tight in the neck with a false arch, on the forehand, and without any brilliance.

*In piaffe: bringing the horse into position with the seat, keeping shoulders, arms, and hands relaxed. Nadine Kloser on the pony gelding Chuck.*

A correct piaffe is a proud, diagonal movement on the spot. Many riders are under the misconception that they must be very active in the saddle to create these collected steps. The opposite is the case. The necessary work must be done in advance so that you can allow a horse to piaffe with nobility and energy. It is too late to start at the piaffe! Classical dressage offers a wealth of gymnastic exercises that optimally prepare the horse for this movement. But that is another subject. Here, I want to focus on the rider's seat as best I can. You should be very straight in the piaffe, with shoulders down and back, and the navel pushed slightly toward the hands. The arms should be allowed to fall loosely and end in relaxed wrists and fingers. Any tension in the shoulders, arms, and hands can take the joy from the horse and his steps will get "sticky." You should reward energetic steps by softening the reins. In this way, you will motivate the horse to even more beautiful steps. Your legs must be just as relaxed as your arms. They hug the horse's body gently and give a command only if the horse is about to quit. This signal comes from a loose, long leg that is *not* pulled up and back, and that picks up the horse in the moment when you have more contact with the leg on the body. This is the correct moment, but please only as needed so that the horse isn't demotivated. My tip: You can best feel this moment wearing jodhpur breeches without tall riding boots. The thick leather of the boot's shaft distances you too much from the horse's body and takes away the sensitivity that you can feel with long breeches. You get a much closer and softer feel of the horse's body.

Positive core tension in the upper body is essential. It helps you to carry your own head instead of letting it bob in the rhythm of the piaffe. With sensitive horses, just "stretching yourself up more" is enough to take them, for example, out of the halt

The rider's head should not protrude forward and nod with the rhythm like a bobble-head doll, either at the trot or in the piaffe. This not only impacts the seat and its effect, it is also unattractive.

or collected steps into the exercise. Such horses can later start to piaffe purely "from the abdomen." The foundation for a beautiful piaffe is a quiet seat that doesn't wiggle around or chase the horse out of his proud steps, which happens when the rider lacks feeling for the rhythm.

Allow your horse to "grow big" in front. Picture horses with a powerful forehand. Let the neck of the horse grow large and noble out of the trunk, and lengthen your reins accordingly. This allows the horse's shoulders to move freely and his front legs develop impressive movement. At the same time, think about short, sinking hindquarters. Imagine that your horse grows in front of you and becomes short and lower behind while you sit on a high, collected back. The

power of imagination can help your seat do the right thing when you practice these upper-level exercises. Look at many photos of good riders on horses that piaffe correctly, and internalize the seat of these examples. Especially make note of the arms, the contour of the back, and the position of the legs.

*Bring your navel a little forward and let the horse piaffe from your abdomen. Julika Tabertshofer on the Quarter Horse gelding QB.*

Piaffe should look light and effortless. A light hand and a sensitive leg are possible when the rider's seat is trained and effective. Anja Beran on Favory Toscana.

The passage carries the rider up and forward in an even wave.

If you wish to ride a classical piaffe, you should never ride with short reins, the neck of the horse deep, or the throatlatch narrow because that decreases the freedom of the forehand. Your horse will lie heavy on the shoulders and can never be brilliant. Also, lose the notion that your legs have to be put far back to build power. This will only end in thrashing steps, which is anything but the picture of an ideal classical piaffe. Inner quiet and relaxation of the rider is a prerequisite for a correct seat in the piaffe.

*To repeat: a well-coordinated body must have significant positive tension in the trunk with a supple pelvis and loose arms and legs. Not an easy combination!*

It is ideal when you can piaffe on multiple horses that know the movement well— to just sit on the horse and learn to feel the movement.

It is very important that you don't "waddle" back and forth in the saddle during the piaffe, but think more about up and down. If you move around there is the danger that you will put the horse into the feared balancé. In this state, the horse throws himself—or maybe just the hindquarters—around, shifting toward the left and toward the right with every step, instead of bending his hocks and accepting the weight.

## The Seat in the Passage

This movement makes greater demands on the seat and experience of the rider because the distinct forward tendency of this noble trot-like movement "throws" the rider more than the piaffe does. The forward impulsion of the hind legs goes up over the horse's back directly into the saddle and requires an elastic adaptation to this movement, since it feels much bigger than the motion in the piaffe. The critical criteria for sitting well in the piaffe also apply to the passage: positive tension in the upper body, and relaxed legs and arms. In contrast to the piaffe, the upper body can be slightly forward to take into account the forward movement. If you sit in the piaffe with a tendency for the shoulders to be back a little, sitting this way in a powerful passage would put you behind the movement.

*In the transition to the passage, the rider's sternum should be taken lightly forward. Vera Munderloh on Favory Toscana.*

*Imagine that you suck the saddle up instead of letting the movement escape forward.*

I imagine that my sternum is slightly forward, especially when I start the passage from a walk or from the piaffe. In order to be able to follow the passage well and to make it more expressive, I recommend that my students imagine that they "suck the saddle up" with the seat.

You should be carried on a wave: steep upward, then floating forward and slowly back down.

The more energetically the horse passages, the more you should lower the hands and yield with the reins. In this way, he can fully use his neck and the forehand will show greater action, while a light impulse from the legs activates the hindquarters. This impulse can be given with the calf, but more precisely with a spur. This has the effect of holding the horse back and encourages the hind leg to step with more expression upward and forward, and not faster. The proper use of the spurs must be learned and requires many years of training so that they don't become a senseless "plague" on the horse. During the movement, it is important to be able to accurately use the spur so that you aren't causing

*The powerful stallion Regedor in the passage under Anja Beran.*

*A stress-free pirouette: Regedor is responding to the rider's seat.*

the horse to lose the rhythm, but rather to support him as necessary. Consequently, you must check the mobility of your ankles now and then.

*Without supple and coordinated ankles, it is impossible to use spurs with precision.*

Many mistakes arise in the passage if the rider is subject to the mistaken belief that she must lift the forehand of the horse through a rhythmical upward action of the hands. This causes an unattractive and agitated picture. A horse that is constantly irritated and blocked with the hands can't passage with energy and expression. Such a horse also has a tight back, which, consequently, "throws" the rider instead of letting her sit. As in the piaffe, tak-ing the leg back and up is an excessive aid that results in an agitated thrashing tail instead of a powerful passage.

Often a piaffe forward is "sold" as a passage, where the hind leg is brought a little forward under the horse's body and the horse minces forward instead of lifting into a powerful hov-ering state. This hovering alone does not make a classical passage because the hind leg stay-ing longer in the air delays the trot sequence and creates an artificial hover moment with a tightly held back. The forward movement is, in this case, much less than with a classical passage because the hind leg is raised more but is taken forward only a little. This artificial passage has lost the desired movement. This means that the rider isn't invited to float with the horse, but rather, she sits on a tight back and gets tossed up and down. This form of movement is equally strenuous and uncom-fortable for rider and horse, and leads to injury for both over a long time of intensive work. In summary, I can say that a correct, supple seat is only possible when the horse does the exercise correctly, because ultimately, he must allow the rider to sit.

Unfortunately, experienced riders often use their hands and legs like a vise, and bore into the horse's back with their seat. It can even look good. But it isn't how it should be. I am talking about a balanced, supple seat that softly accompanies the horse during the exercise and requires erect posture and relax-ation from the rider. It's a seat that keeps the horse's back healthy and also prevents dam-age to the rider.

The pirouette showing the rider's eyes slightly to the inside of the horse's shoulder and the horse bending well. Vera Munderloh on Super.

The rider's trunk turns the horse in the pirouette, like closing a clicking screw cap of a bottle.

## The Seat in the Canter Pirouette

The pirouette is one of the most difficult exercises of all and tolerates no disturbance from the rider's seat. There can be no forceful pushing in the saddle during the shortened canter stride that the pirouette requires. You must sit as quietly as possible, maximally upright with a little more weight in the inside stirrup and the inside seat bone. Just with that you suggest the pirouette and the direction to the horse. The pirouette demands extreme patience and feel from the rider. Only a few riders are able to wait on the horse, to accompany him quietly in the rotation around the hindquarters and enjoy the pirouette. Instead, we

see riders drive constantly—out of fear that the horse will stop at any moment—so the horse jumps sideways: with a lot of action from the hand, spurs, and upper body, the rider tries to lift the forehand and pull the horse around.

But here, *less is more*. Happy is the rider who has the courage to be passive and can lead her horse with a light hand. Now is precisely when the psychological aspects come into play and influence the seat enormously. The rider who is calm and completely with her horse allows the pirouette to happen. The one who is afraid that the exercise isn't going to work or wants to do it especially well and is, consequently, nervous, can never achieve the relaxed seat necessary for the pirouette and will hurry her horse

with unnecessary aids. The pirouette is not an exercise where you can improve things. The foundation work must be worked out in advance, meaning obedience to the leg, the horse's sensitive response to the seat, and lightness in the hand. In the pirouette, you reap what you have previously sown, and are, therefore, allowed to enjoy it!

Looking over the horse's inside shoulder helps to prepare your body well for the pirouette, and you are automatically correctly turned. The outside rein works softly against the neck and presses the forehand around while your inside hand leads the horse sideways. With many horses, the strides are more expressive if you lift the inside hand a little. Bring your shoulders well back because you don't want a canter

*A powerful Spanish Walk with the hands being held a bit higher. Silvia Wimmer on Quilate.*

stride forward, only to the side. Your shoulders should be oriented to those of the horse. Your inside calf lies near the girth and maintains the bend and impulsion of the canter stride, while the outside is taken slightly back and controls the hindquarters. We often see the error of the outside spur agitating the horse near the saddle pad, with the lower leg bent from the knee and pulled high. This is not just ineffective, but also unattractive and it disturbs the whole seat. A long, outside leg that is simply brought back a little is recommended for the pirouette.

Your upper body must be erect and held quietly. Under no circumstances should you tip forward or backward because this will easily bring the horse behind the aids, and the pirouette will creep along or the horse might throw himself around. Erect posture is necessary to keep the horse on the aids.

## The Seat in the Spanish Walk

The horse's balance is very fragile in the Spanish walk because there is no impulsion. The lack of tempo makes a balancing act out of carrying the foreleg horizontally in the air as the diagonal hind leg lifts off. Consequently, the rider's seat must not disturb the horse. Many riders tend to shift their weight side to side in the saddle, thinking that gives more freedom to the corresponding front leg. This is unattractive to watch, and causes the horse to sway or crossover.

You must strive for a still upper body and hands that are held as quietly as possible. Many horses require a slightly higher hand. This varies and must be determined indi-

*Sit straight, keep the hands at the same level, and don't disturb the balance. Anja Beran on Regedor.*

vidually. Alternating raising of the hand is distracting and you shouldn't get in the habit of it. When you want the right front leg to extend, your diagonal left leg should activate the horse's hind leg to step forward, while your leg on the same side prevents the croup from evading. It helps most horses to lift your seat bone on the same side to free up their shoulder. This must be done very subtly or the horse will start swerving unacceptably. You should also watch out that you don't stretch out your own head when the horse is in the Spanish walk. First, it doesn't help the exercise, and second, it doesn't look good.

To be done well, the Spanish walk requires a high degree of calm and coordination from the rider.

## Using the Seat to Straighten a Horse

After analyzing where a horse is stiff and where he is hollow, you can use seat aids to straighten the horse. Many horses' movement shoves the saddle and the rider's weight away from the hollow side. This is especially visible on circles and voltes when the inside is the horse's hollow side. This requires you to purposefully step inside and down. You must "sit against" and not allow the horse to shift you to the outside. Over time, this causes the saddle to become crooked, which makes it even more difficult to sit in the middle. The rider must be so well trained in the sensitivity of the seat that she can perceive this crookedness, and she must be coordinated enough to maintain a correct position despite it, and give correct aids.

If, for example, a horse carries his neck very hollow to the left and likes to move his croup to the left, the rider going to the left must carry her inside left leg a little farther back than the outside leg. This puts her in position to control the hindquarters and prevent an evasion to the left. The right hand asks for a slight counter-positioning and is against the neck in order to press the horse's shoulders slightly to the left, bringing the shoulders in front of the hindquarters. The left hand is carried a little to the inside to show the horse the way, for example, through a corner or on a circle. The rider should align her upper body so that her shoulders are on the line of travel. This sounds very simple and doable. But I am talking about advanced riding here. It isn't so easy to flex your horse, for example to the right, while you have to turn yourself a little left in order to ride the line of the circle in counter-flexion. My students often have huge difficulties with this due to insufficient body control.

When a horse is stiff on the right side, it is helpful to ride a lot of shoulder-fore or shoulder-in in this direction to make the horse straight and supple. This works better for many riders. Nevertheless, many riders tend to hold the rein the horse won't soften on too tightly. They cramp their whole arm and shoulder. We must always remember that *giving* followed by a renewed request for bend and flexion, are the keys to success.

*A horse can't lean on a loose rein!*

You should constantly think about all of your physical movements on the horse: Are they really necessary? Were they too strong? Did they last too long? Were they at the right moment?

## Holding the Whip

The rider should be able to use the whip equally well in either hand. Many riders have a preferred "whip hand" that is more agile than the other. If you notice such an asymmetry, you should force yourself to train holding the whip in both the left *and* the right hand. Naturally, the decision as to where you carry the whip depends on the horse's training, but you must develop the ability to use it equally well with both wrists. Later, when you ride with one hand, the whip must be carried in the right hand.

When the whip isn't correctly placed, it can constantly touch the croup of the horse, making him sullen and dull. The whip is used from a relaxed wrist without letting go of the reins. Disturbing the horse's mouth when using the whip must be strictly avoided. Consequently, it is very important to not use the whole arm in the action but merely the wrist and the fingers.

The knob of the whip should not extend any farther out of the rein fist than necessary to assure a secure grip. A handle that sticks up too far can potentially result in injury to the rider.

Changing the whip from one side to the other should be almost not noticed by the horse and, above all, should not affect the fluidity of movement. A young horse must get used to this. When first trying to change the whip to the other hand, an assistant should hold him. It is elegant and practical if you can first put the reins and the whip in one hand, then grab the whip with the other, move it in a half circle over to the other side, and immediately take up the reins again.

If the whip isn't too long, you can also pull it out and forward as if it were a sword and take it to the other side.

The whip is in the right hand resting across the thigh. Anja Beran on Campeao.

The whip rests on the thigh of the rider. This is critical because only in this position is it assured that the rider's wrist remains correctly positioned. When the whip points vertically down at the horse's shoulder, the rider's wrist is bent. The same is true when the whip is carried at the rider's waist, meaning much too high. If the whip isn't carried properly, the correct straight line from the elbow over the wrist is interrupted. You can check for yourself if your whip is truly on the thigh and if your hand position is correct.

*A slip-on spur bent up and in is worn right above the heel.*

*Strap-on spurs sit quite a bit higher than the slip-on spur.*

*Straight slip-on spurs are put on just above the heel.*

## How to Use the Spur

Only someone who can sit relaxed without clamping the legs and has supple ankles and controlled leg aids should attempt to use spurs. Riders must be trained with expert instruction about their use. The naïve thought that spurs make a lazy, dull horse energetic and sensitive is an illusion. There are many ways to learn to use this tool. The horse must accept them if riding with spurs isn't to become a primitive subject for the rider and a painful one for the horse. As always, it's a balanced seat and coordinated legs that enable the rider of good will to use spurs with feeling and respect.

Spurs worn high on hard riding boots make it difficult for riders to use them with feeling. The horse's body can feel a little hard and solid when riding in tall riding boots. You can get nowhere with a light play of the ankle when the spur sits too high.

This is why Udo Bürger recommended the following in his book *The Way to Perfect Horsemanship*:

*"One gets the correct feel when wearing long riding breeches with the spurs on the edge of a low shoe directly on the tendon of the heel that is* only covered by socks. This does away with any overly strong use automatically."

Conforming with this advice, I recommend to my students that they wear jodhpur pants and slip-on spurs on jodhpur boots. They sit down low, directly above the heel of the boot and allow a mobile ankle and precise use. Jodhpur pants allow a soft hug of the leg on the horse's body and contribute to the sensitivity of the rider.

The choice of spur depends on one hand on the length of the rider's leg, and on the other hand, on the sensitivity and curvature of the ribs of the horse. It is better to ride very thin-skinned horses with blunt spurs. Thick-skinned horses, not so easily aroused, can better be kept sensitive to the leg with spurs that are a little sharper or have rowels. The most important thing is to not "dull" the horse. Consequently, the use of spurs must be very precise and measured and should get an immediate reaction from the horse. A phlegmatic horse is often given to riders with little experience and without a good seat because he seems safe. However, if you want such a horse well exercised and sensitively ridden, you need a rider with an effective seat and superlative leg position.

The horse must be touched up with spurs to make him brilliant again rather than dull.

When the rider is very large with legs that hang below the horse's body, the length of leg requires spurs that are curved up. To avoid an undesirable lift of the heel, it is recommended to wear spurs with a swan neck to be able to comfortably touch the horse at the appropriate spot. For riders with very short legs, it is just the opposite, because they tend to have their heels in constant contact with the horse's body. These riders should use spurs that are either short or curved down to avoid inadvertent use of them. When the curvature of the horse's ribs is especially wide, a rider often has trouble putting the spurs on the horse: she must turn her toes out. In this case, spurs that are bent to the inside solve the problem.

If you are to use spurs intentionally, you must always be conscious of exactly where your leg is. You must know if you have it in a forward- or sideways-driving position, or if it is merely in a guarding position. Furthermore, your leg should be so quiet and coordinated that you are able to use the spur merely on the hair against the direction of hair growth. You can practice this when the horse is standing still and you have the eyes

*Slip-on spurs bent up and in. They allow touching the horse without turning the foot.*

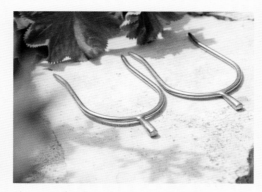

*Short, straight, slip-on spurs.*

*Slip-on spurs bent inward. These are only appropriate for very advanced riders. The danger is great that the horse will be touched without the rider knowing it.*

of an expert on you. It is helpful to imagine an exact gradation on the horse's body to signal particular responses and movements. On one spot you bring the horse into the piaffe, a breath of a touch on another spot signals the horse to canter, while another spot indicates passage. These "points" are only a few inches apart or it would not be possible to ride with invisible aids.

You can now understand why well-trained horses are rare and why they are so easily ruined. Understandably, the movements are not the only use for spurs, as they are a part of the interplay of the aids. The exact and sensitive use of spurs has a decisive influence on the success of a movement and the brilliance of the horse. Few horses are electric off the leg. Nor are there many that are not subject to a rider's constant nagging and that present themselves at the highest level with eagerness and pride.

*The spur is an excellent means of getting more expression out of the horse, also to ask for many different movements through just a touch at different points. You can't be as precise with just the calf.*

Unfortunately, when a rider with insufficient training uses the spur inexpertly, it can cause rough treatment of the horse and, ultimately, make him dull. Bare patches of skin where riders without any sensitivity monotonously and constantly beat against the horse's body are a sad sign of the inability of the rider. With correct use of spurs there are no such skin irritations on the horse's body that can sometimes develop into thick "leathery" skin.

A spur should never be used with the lower leg pulled back and up. If you see a rider using spurs near the saddle pad, you will also see a horse that swats his tail, eventually even kicking against the spur with a hind leg, laying his ears back, and throwing his head up. Using the spurs too far back and up always gets a big negative reaction and never leads to fine communication between horse and rider.

Before you use spurs, check whether you are really able to move your leg a few inches as needed from the hip, or whether you simply take the leg back and up from the knee. In the latter case, you should definitely work on your seat with an experienced riding instructor and correct your leg position until you are out of this bad habit.

Finally, you should learn from your instructor the most important ways of using a spur and practice the different options with a supple ankle, preferably on a still horse.

As an aid, the spur softly touches the horse to signal what the rider wants. It can also be used with tiny, lightning-fast touches to wake a horse up if you feel that he isn't alert. During a movement the spur can carefully tickle to remind the horse to maintain his carriage and to keep going. A discreet but slightly longer touch with light pressure on the right spot can give a movement more impulsion and expression. A shorter, surprising stab can be a punishment and should rarely be used.

Sometimes it can be necessary to "pinch" with the spur if the horse, for example, is leaning against it. To do this, you apply the spur slowly and with increasing pressure. As soon as you sense that the horse is active and lifts the back, meaning he responds to the spur, stop the pinch and release the horse. Naturally, the rider must be able to use this aid precisely on the spot and at the right moment, which requires an independent and relaxed seat, a mobile ankle, and a lot of feel.

It is helpful to imagine that a hind leg hangs from each spur. You don't want to just make the leg move "faster," but to lift it farther up—for example, in a transition from trot to passage. I must always be conscious of all these possibilities of using the spurs. With advanced practice, the use of spurs will become intuitive.

In battle, horses were trained to back up when the spurs were used at the girth on both sides. This left the hands free to fight while getting out of the way of the enemy. A sharp halt from a canter was also commanded by pressing the spurs on both sides. The spurs bring the hind legs under the center of gravity to get a stop with bent hocks.

Bending and flexing a horse can often be supported with a light touch of the spur on the desired spot. Above all, the inside spur frequently contributes to good bend, beautiful elevation, and energetic forward movement in the half-pass.

You can see that riding with spurs is an art and can have many uses. I hope that the naïve thought that a horse is made more energetic and runs faster with spurs is dispelled and that every rider will get trained in the use of the spurs in order to not hurt her horse.

*Note: No horse naturally reacts as desired to the spurs.*

It never ceases to amaze me how many riders think the spur instantly gets a positive reflex from the horse. This is completely false. A horse must be taught about the spurs and what the desired response is so that the correct reaction is strengthened and the incorrect reactions that you often get at the beginning are negated. These include behaviors like kicking at the spur, tensing, holding or cramping, going backward, twitching the skin, and pressing against the spurs, to mention only a few.

How to train a horse to spurs is out of the scope of this book. I want to focus on the correct spur aids from a good seat with supple ankles.

## Taking Up the Reins

Out of respect for the horse's mouth, I sit straight when I pick up the reins and establish a soft contact. You should not lean forward and pull on the head and neck of the horse. Do not use muscular energy when picking up the reins! Once again the mentality of the rider plays out in the seat: Are you relaxed enough to develop a soft contact with your horse and then to shape him in the

course of the exercise? Or do you demand a prompt yield by the horse? Are you thinking if the horse doesn't yield "softly" then you can use the strength necessary? Whoever has this idea will have a hard time achieving an elegant seat and a harmonious picture with her horse.

*The rider who can wait can sit more elegantly and relaxed.*

If you have a lot of feel for your horse and are calm, you can act with loose arms and wrists. If you want to force your horse into a frame and have in your mind a "silhouette" of a highly trained horse, your arms will tense and you will force the rounding of the neck with stiff wrists and muscle power. Locking the arms always causes your shoulders to tense and your back to stiffen and the whole seat loses relaxation.

## How to Use the Curb Bit and the Bridoon

Working with four reins requires experience and feel. Be conscious of the lifting effect of the snaffle and the rounding effect of the curb to avoid mistakes in the use of the different reins. Knowledge of theory and focused training in riding with a curb and bridoon will quickly lead to success. Many riders beginning to ride with the curb stiffen in the seat and stick the arms forward because they don't want to make any mistakes. Try to avoid doing this and stay natural and loose sitting on your horse.

It is very helpful to drop the reins now and then, and pick them up again to gain experience in how to hold the reins and tell the reins apart. Have a riding instructor check your shoulder and arm position regularly to avoid negative changes when riding with a curb. Meet the new challenge playfully:

Imagine that you can direct your horse with loose fingers. Arms and wrists aren't necessary any more—only the fingers cause your horse to chew, soften the lower jaw, and you can develop a fine connection to him. The weight in your hand should not exceed the weight of the leather of the reins. Nevertheless, the horse maintains a light contact with you without leaning on your hands or pulling. You can never sit well and balanced if your horse is lying on your hand or pulling down/forward because that requires a lot of tension in your body to counteract this pull, which destroys your balance.

I recommend to my students that they use thin reins. If you are really committed to direct your horse with the lightest movement of the fingers, it is much easier to do it with thin reins. I strictly advise against the bad habit of riding with a curb bit using heavy reins or with stops on the bridoon reins. This rein has its place when jumping or trail riding, but in upper-level dressage, a rein should flow smoothly through the fingers. This is impossible with the hard stops.

How you hold the reins is not important to the horse as long as you are respectful and careful with the bits. You should quietly practice the different possibilities of divided rein holds, including Fillis's variations and the classical 3:1, to see what works best for you. When you are constantly busy focusing on sorting out the reins your seat will suffer. Your seat should be so secure and quiet that you are truly able to sit "rein independent." Otherwise, it is too soon to ride with a curb bit.

It is important to me to note that the rein fist must remain as quiet as possible. The curb rein, which is fastened to a shank bit, should be symmetrical and the snaffle reins are constantly dominant. Although it will never be perfected, I regularly resolve that I will only move the rein hands to the side or up, or close the fingers to stop, but never take my hands back.

*The reins should always be used carefully! Here, you see contact on the snaffle reins while the curb reins hang loose.*

I had a trainer that placed a lot of value on this and was always watching my hands. Just the desire and the visual in mind of riding this way can be extremely helpful and greatly encourages an effective seat. The less I use my hands, the more I have to focus on aids from the seat. Now we come to another point in my riding development that helped me a lot: all of the movements that I could ride with rein contact, I would practice once an hour without contact, and most importantly, introduce the movement without contact. This wasn't easy to do and I experimented a lot with how I needed to use my seat in order to tell my horse what we were going to do next. That was the moment when I learned to "let go" in the truest sense of the words.

As humans we are driven to do everything with our hands. We grab, pull, touch, press, and strike with them in all situations in our life. Large signs saying, "Please don't touch," are there to stop us from picking up an object to better understand what we can plainly see. Because it is human nature, the exact same thing happens on the horse. In the beginning stages, we hold on tight to the reins and don't think about the fact that on the other end, a metal piece is in the sensitive mouth of the horse. Later, we want to influence and control the large animal by pulling on the reins, jerking, and squeezing the fists. It gives us a good (meaning secure) feeling if we have a stable contact with the horse's mouth, make the horse's neck round, and have immediate control when our hand acts. Many of these things are unconscious. You might not want to pull when the horse starts trotting fast, but we do it reflexively. Therefore, it is important that we become aware of this and think a lot about what our hands are doing—and watch them painstakingly.

Riding advanced movements without rein contact can help a lot and shows us possibilities of communication with the seat that we never considered before. Of course, the horse's neck will be a little longer and the jaw a little more open, meaning less on the bit, but that isn't important. The question you want to clarify is: are you able to ride a pirouette almost exclusively from the seat? A piaffe or passage? Or are you merely a "hand rider"? The test of the upper-level movements without rein contact is not just a milestone in the development of your seat. It is an excellent test of whether or not your horse is balanced (collected), because it won't happen when the horse is on the forehand! It is also extremely positive for your horse and will increase balance, self-confidence, and motivation when he can present himself "independently" without the restrictions of the reins.

*We are now at the point that we want to reach with every horse, regardless of the discipline for which he is being trained: the horse carries himself.*

A so-called loss of connection, assuming it is due to the rider and not the horse, is something to strive for, and it is incorrect that it is punished today in dressage tests with the loss of points. It has always been the goal of training to be able to direct the horse from the seat and to present him in proud self-carriage. As Udo Bürger says:

*"Contact is more praiseworthy the less there is of it. If I can ride a whole dressage test without rein contact, with the horse beyond reproach in gait, swing, carriage, and obedience to the aids, the horse is beautifully on the seat and it can't be better than that.*

*"Occasionally taking up connection to the mouth, of whatever degree, is then just a reminder for the horse that indicates to him that 'you should watch the carriage!' The dressage horse should be allowed to lengthen, chewing the reins out of the hand, and flex at the poll when you allow it from the seat and posture, and not merely because you give up the contact."*

The Way to Perfect Horsemanship by Udo Bürger (Trafalgar Square Books, 2012)

Make note of the fact that the more I release contact with the hand the more I need the seat. If we want to improve, the hand must be used as a nice accessory and not as the primary aid, as is almost always the case today when I watch at a riding arena.

*Allow the horse to release from the seat—then both rider and horse relax. Nadine Kloser and Chuck.*

*It should be our goal to have a horse that is dependent on our seat and independent of our hand!*

# A BRIEF DISCUSSION OF **BREATHING**

*"While performing the movements, the rider must breathe deeply so that all goes without tension or fatigue, and without the motion being choppy. Everything she does transfers to the horse, the good as well as the bad."*

*Notizen zum Unterricht* (Instruction notes) by Nuno Oliveira (Olms Verlag, 1998)

Time and again, I see riders' faces change color as they ride. They take on a stone-face look, because their breathing is flat and irregular. This can have various causes, such as fear or simply concentrating too hard. Not breathing well puts our body under stress, making it difficult to sit relaxed and focused in the saddle, and to react with flexibility. Deep and quiet breathing is very important during physical activity because the body needs oxygen for energy. The muscles need oxygen to be able to work optimally. Consequently, it is important that the instructor and the rider herself often check whether she is breathing freely. When there are consistent issues, it is generally beyond the role of the riding instructor to improve the prob-

lem—the student should be encouraged to work on her breathing on her own. It is important also to practice correct breathing out of the saddle. When I see that someone has difficulties breathing free and deep, I recommend they seek a breathing therapist, because a relaxed seat is never possible with restricted breathing.

Many riders tend to breathe fast and short with harder work, such as cantering. Breathing flat means the air is merely pushed in and out of the upper part of the respiratory tract without getting down to the lower respiratory tract and to the lungs, where the gas exchange takes place. Consequently, there is not enough supply of oxygen.

In our barn, we have a former opera singer who teaches us riders many exercises so we can breathe quietly and deeply all the time, even in stressful situations. I first learned about the importance of breathing through painstaking work with the classical singer Gerda Prochaska-Stolze. It is something that should function without us thinking about it. It happens—like the tendency of humans to do everything with the hands—unconsciously.

We need to be conscious of how we are breathing, because in a crisis, we frequently fail to breathe. When I noticed that some riders were dizzy after the initial breathing exercises with Gerda Prochaska-Stolze, it was clear to me that we apparently don't exhaust the possibilities of our breathing and that there is much to improve.

In my own case, I have found that good breathing technique improves my ability to talk loudly for hours like I have to when giving riding lessons. It is easier on my voice, the sound is more pleasant for listeners, and I can maintain a louder volume without straining. The diaphragm works correctly with good breathing training. This elastic muscle pulls on the last ribs toward the upper abdomen when breathing in. This is an important training concept that is always integrated into deep breathing. Singers and actors can hold a note even with tremolo, and can fill a large hall with their voice without technical assistance when breathing from the diaphragm!

It is ideal for deep breathing to become automatic so that you do it all day long, as well as when riding. It can help you a lot on the horse, especially when you are on a very tense horse. It also helps to breathe deeply with regularity to signal to the horse that all is in order and there is no need to be upset. This calmness also translates to the seat and then again to the horse. Gerda Prochaska-Stolze says:

*"Singers and actors practice deep breathing for years. It provides the elixir of life—oxygen—to the body and the mind, and is important for circulation to the brain. Deep breathing relaxes you in stressful situations and gives you the chance to react appropriately. This can be extremely helpful on a horse and can be a major contribution to the safety of horse and rider. To learn deep breathing you need a trainer to work with you at least once a week. It isn't learned in a short amount of time, but takes about half a year of instruction before you can finally practice it independently. Deep breathing opens a new way to release and relax when riding and can be varied from lesson to lesson. With well-trained breathing, your body and mind are fit and receptive.*

*"Also, when you are stressed from your day at the office as you come to the barn, you can relax yourself with breathing exercises. Even five minutes of controlled breathing outside, assuming the air isn't too cold, can help diminish stress and worries. In this way, you can approach your horse free and relaxed, and nothing stands in the way of enjoying the ride together."*

Note:

*The classical singer, mezzo soprano Gerda Prochaska-Stolze was born in Brunn, Austria, and moved to Garmisch-Partenkirchen in 1949. She trained with Professor Kuhn-Englder before entering the conservatory in Vienna. Later, she was engaged for a long time at the Volks Opera of Vienna. She is married to chamber singer Gerhard Stolze.*

It is important to note that deep and quiet breathing is only possible with erect posture. No one can breathe freely when slouching on a chair. Likewise, you cannot breathe freely if you sit on a horse with a rounded back and the head jutting out. If you want to work on your breathing, you must also improve your posture.

But be careful. You must work with an expert. Go to a singing teacher or someone that teaches at an acting school, or a trained breathing therapist. Only then will you get correct instruction. For the first several months you should practice the breathing exercises only under the eye of an instructor. Later, you will be able to practice on your own. You must check regularly that you are doing it correctly. Conscious deep breathing must be developed and practiced over years, and isn't something that you can quickly imitate or experience with a few tips.

Additionally, you should never practice breathing training outside in very cold temperatures or in a strong wind, although it is generally very good to practice in fresh air— just not with extreme weather conditions.

A basic exercise is to stand straight with the legs hip-width apart. In this position, you can breathe in as long and deep as possible while gradually lifting the arms straight up. It is important that the volume of the abdomen distinctly enlarges. Then let the air completely out, slowly, through the mouth while you let the arms fall down and stretch the fingertips to the ground. The volume of the abdomen must reduce again correspondingly. Later, this very slow exhale should be done through the mouth and intermittently in a defined rhythm. After a long time training, you should be able to do this regardless of whether you are moving around slowly or fast. This develops the ability to breathe deeply, independently of other physical actions.

*Breathing is an important factor in developing body perception and control and, therefore, deserves significant attention!*

# **PSYCHOLOGICAL** ASPECTS

Your mental state influences your body posture and muscle tension. The utility of your seat is dependent on how you feel. This has been known a long time. In the afterword of Gustav Steinbrecht's famous work *The Gymnasium of the Horse*, there is a comprehensive overview of the factors that are critical to being a good rider, without mentioning how difficult it is to achieve.

To understand the influence of your psychology on your seat, I would like to digress a little first and go into the special things about the art of riding that you should strive for if you are privileged to sit on the back of a horse. Steinbrecht says:

"No art has the extensive, various, and complex difficulties to wrestle with as does the art of riding. Special complex requirements are placed not just on the rider practicing the art, but also on the instrument that she uses, namely the horse. There are also many limitations in teaching to overcome.

"To support this assertion, I will compare the art of riding with other arts and follow the thought process developed by a famous French riding master who is still a recognized authority in France: General l'Hotte.

"First, the one learning the art, the student, must bring so many capabilities together—the body, the character, and the mind—as nature only seldom provides to an individual person.

No other art requires as much from its students. Unlike painters, sculptors, or musicians that require trained arms and hands to achieve their art, the correct rider must use the whole body, arms, legs, and muscles coordinated together when riding.

"Additionally, there are special characteristics that must be developed, namely calm with energy, relaxation without weakness, and firmness without roughness. Moreover, the rider must have such self-control so she is constantly master of her emotional expressions, countering impatience with patience, temper with calm, lethargy and disobedience with determination. Free of vanity, her enthusiasm for the art must rest on a certain ethical stability that discour-

*agement can't shatter and no difficulty can sway. The correct rider must demonstrate perseverance more than any other artist.*

*"These physical and personality characteristics must be expanded by a full understanding of the scientific principles of riding theory, so that the rider can perform all the processes in riding and use all the knowledge learned, first in the saddle and then as an instructor.*

*"When such huge and necessary preconditions are fulfilled, the most important is still to come: namely the right feel—a rider's sensitive tact."*

The Gymnasium of the Horse by Gustav Steinbrecht (Xenophon Press, 2014)

Even back then, it was recognized that a good rider is not simply trained, and that many aspects influence the supple seat and its measured effect on the equine partner. Body, character, mind, and feeling are the four pillars that lead to success. Consequently, the riding art forms the student in the extreme and influences her whole being, but only if she is ready to work on it constantly. We should use this opportunity to apply ourselves and develop our personality. It is remarkable how improving our inner attitude has a positive influence on our seat.

If you come to the barn stressed and tense, your horse will feel that you aren't "with him" and will, likewise, react stressed. It is very important that you try to relax before you get to the barn. This can be achieved with breathing exercises, yoga, or other gymnastic or relaxation techniques. Each of us must figure out what works best for us. But first, we must realize what state we are in. This self-awareness is a prerequisite for improving something. I often discover that my riding students aren't aware how nervous, distracted, or tense they are. The horse mirrors their current emotional state and a vicious cycle begins: Horse and rider rub off on each other! The horse moves in tension, the rider can't possibly sit well, which causes the horse to brace, and finally, the riding lesson ends with a great deal of frustration for both.

Try to always go to your horse with joy and shake off negative thoughts. Try to free yourself to focus on your horse.

*Ultimately, you can only have a clear perception of your horse if you also know yourself.*

Fear in the saddle is a huge subject. If you are afraid, admit it, and talk about it with your riding instructor in order to avoid expectations being set too high. Let her know what you are comfortable with and what you aren't. There is no shame in that. Don't put yourself under pressure and don't think you must prove something. That will have a negative effect on your seat.

Fear makes you sit cramped and cowering on the horse. The constant expectation that something bad is going to happen makes you hold the reins short and tight. Holding the horse "tight" with the hand in combination with a tight seat will upset the horse, giving the rider the feeling that he also expects something terrible to happen. Again, a vicious cycle!

A mellow school horse can help give self-confidence, since he isn't so easily influenced by the emotions of the rider, and trust can develop. An anxious rider must have a quiet school horse. Recognize your fear, talk about it, and ride only what you are comfortable with. During this work you should try to breathe calmly and consciously to achieve a supple seat. Check your length of rein and your hands now and then. Are they tense? When you feel comfortable and trust your horse, you should try to raise the expectations. You must not canter or jump if you don't feel you are ready. If you try it anyway, it might lead to a bad experience.

Riding demands honesty and knowing your emotions!

*Close your eyes to shut out all the visual, environmental stimuli and concentrate fully on feeling the horse: Nadine Kloser on Chuck.*

Many riders arrive at the barn after a long day's work feeling aggressive and impatient, and they need a boxing bag more than an extremely sensitive living being to interact with.

Horses that carry such riders are to be pitied. The riders generally sit hard in the saddle and fiddle away with hands and legs using a lot of strength. They wait for a small loss of attention or a mistake by the horse to unload all their stored-up anger on them. When in such a mood, they cannot sit in the saddle in a supple and elegant way. They will be stiff and ride with a harsh expression. If they easily get in such an emotional condition, they should never get on a horse. They should longe their horse or ask a barn colleague to ride the horse. The damage to their horse's trust that they will cause in an out-of-control moment is much worse than if they didn't ride their horse that day.

It is our greatest challenge to encounter our horse every day with a free spirit and a happy mood. Only then are we open to perceive how he is and what work is reasonable for that day. We should train ourselves to understand this and always think about what we can succeed at on a given day.

Patience is another characteristic that is mentioned by Steinbrecht. When someone is impatient, the aids are often too strong, too fast, or given too often. During a passage, for example, the horse won't be able to carry himself with great brilliance, but rather is hurried along in short hover steps. Many riders allow themselves to use the seat and other aids roughly to punish their horse. They are full of impatience and think the horse isn't responding as they want.

Consider that when a horse doesn't do something you want, he might not be physically able to, or he hasn't understood what you want of him. Stay relaxed in the saddle, breathe deeply, quietly repeat the exercise, and reflect! Go through the control points of your seat with an imaginary checklist.

Perhaps the cause is contradictory aids that you aren't aware of, but which prevent your horse from doing what you want. I am an extremely patient person and it doesn't upset me if a horse can't repeat something or does it wrong because I learn a lot in those situations. Almost always, it is not monotonous repetition of an exercise that brings success, but rather thinking about it. Suddenly, you will figure out where the problem is coming from, try another way, and you will immediately feel that now you have success. Mistakes can be the source of new creative ways to expand your equestrian repertoire.

The most important prerequisite for a good seat is the greatest possible inner calm.

Many riders are nervous and can't concentrate because they are thinking about ten things at the same time and fidget around on the horse without knowing in the slightest what their individual arms and legs are doing. Only inner calm enables you to focus on one thing. As a riding instructor, it is difficult to instruct students that are not calm. For example, if I give the direction "carry the outside hand a little higher," something hectic will be done and many body parts are involved in the movement. If you are lucky, the outside hand will be one of them.

I try to calm such riders. They should try to concentrate and be conscious of their body through deep breathing and riding at a quiet tempo. If they can't feel their own body, they can't feel the horse's body. They live in their own busy world full of eagerness to do everything correctly, but that requires understanding about what *is* correct, first. Such riders don't know this, because they are too anxious and are exclusively focused on themselves. It is hard to improve under these circumstances. Calm riders have a much easier time developing a good seat. They wait for a correction and concentrate on trying to follow the instructions exactly. When their coordination allows them to control their body

appropriately, it is possible to learn in a relatively short amount of time to sit relaxed and effectively on a horse.

Many riders, including me, can learn a lot by watching other riders. Look for a place where there is good riding and teach yourself with concentrated observation. You will be able to store away the positive images and to internalize them. Later, when you are on a horse, you can try to imitate what you saw. Imagine a rider who sits very well and copy her seat. Gradually, you will sit better and better. But be careful: you should avoid bad visuals, because, unfortunately, we also unconsciously store bad ones, as well. Turn away when someone is riding poorly and only keep the positive impressions in front of your mental eyes, because only those will help you improve. If you only watch aesthetic riding, you will be able to call up these images when riding and they will help you. Visualization requires concentration and attention to detail. Both are important aspects for improving the seat.

In summary, let's listen to the words of Udo Bürger:

*"To control a living being you must first learn to control yourself. You need to be in a good mood and relaxed for riding. A rider should never feel fear, impatience, or anger. Never look at riding as a duty and don't make yourself a slave for an hour like you are riding to lose weight. If you can, stay joyful, and don't plan every minute in the saddle. Only ride when you can truly enjoy it."*

The Way to Perfect Horsemanship by Udo Bürger (Trafalgar Square Books, 2012)

*Training with joy and spirit. Positive energy lets the horse shine even in difficult exercises. Jana Lacey-Krone on Ramzes.*

# INTRODUCTION TO **PART TWO**

In the following section, you will hear from physiotherapist, dance, and gymnastics instructor Veronika Brod. For five years, I have been working with her to improve my mobility and coordination in dance lessons.

Veronika developed a modern dance warm-up routine for me that comprehensively addresses my problems. The improvements in my posture and mobility are incredible. Many small problems that would pop up due to one-sided loading in riding stopped. When it pulls a little here or there, I now know exactly what gymnastic exercise is necessary, and I can resolve the problem myself. Consequently, I can better understand how the horse feels when he is stiff or crooked and we are asking things from him that he just isn't physically able to do at that moment. Pushing through with harder aids is replaced completely by reflecting and discovering the exercises necessary for success. Anything else causes annoyance and wear and tear.

An additional big advantage of my gymnastic and dance lessons is the ability to better analyze the posture problems of my riding students and to help them correct them. It is just like dancing: suppleness, coordination, posture, and feel, which is much more difficult on a living being than on the parquet floor. When I see the problems I have with dancing because I keep losing coordination and posture, I wonder how we humans can accomplish anything on a horse at all.

After about a year of such positive training with Veronika Brod, I had a key experience. A friend of mine, who is also a rider, wanted to come along. I asked Veronika if we could start taking lessons together. She answered that it depended on the physical ability of my friend and that she first would have to come for a lesson alone. After that she called me and said, "Together? Absolutely not!"

She explained to me that while we would both be learning the same dance steps, the way we would have to learn them was totally different. My friend is very supple, with little muscle tone and not a lot of strength. On the other hand, I have a high degree of muscle tone, am rather stiff and have a lot of strength. Consequently, it was impossible for us to do the same gymnastics and get a good result. My friend needed exercises to strengthen her and to gain more stability, while I needed exercises for stretching and suppleness. Then it was clear to me that it isn't just about "doing gymnastics," but rather that a program must be individualized.

It is the same thing with training horses! Every animal requires his individual training

program—in the warm-up and for the rest of the hour. Every horse also needs additional exercises to become straight and supple.

In the meantime, a very fruitful symbiosis has developed. Veronika studied the problems that many riders have, and she visits us regularly to improve our posture on the horse. As a non-rider, she has a completely different perspective and assists us from the point of view of a physiotherapist and dancer, and we have very good results. Long-term success is only possible, however, when riders work on themselves on their own—that is, practice the exercises regularly and check their posture frequently in the mirror.

Seat and posture aren't a gift and can't be developed quickly. They must be worked on for life! In the words of Udo Bürger:

*"If you feel called to train horses, then start with yourself. You should never feel it is too late to learn the rules of the game and prove yourself worthy of an equine partner as a fair sportsman. Endurance leads to success, as in every sport. Let it be said to the beginners that only a thoroughly trained and gymnastically talented sportsman can do justice to being in the saddle. The rider doesn't build athletic muscles. They have to be developed in a different way. You don't need bulging muscles, but rather taut, steely muscles that are ruled lightning fast by will and react in millimeters. Weaklings injure the lower back, flabby muscles get tight because they don't have any inner strength. If you don't carry your shoulders and arms appropriately in your everyday posture, but put your hands on your back or look for support putting a hand in a pocket, you must first conquer this inner weakness before your body is able to act as the transfer station between driving and holding aids. The musculature that the rider needs is developed in track and field athletics and in posture exercises."*

The Way to Perfect Horsemanship by Udo Bürger (Trafalgar Square Books, 2012)

# THE DRESSAGE SEAT FROM THE
# **PHYSIOTHERAPIST'S POINT OF VIEW**
## Advice for Erect Posture and a Sensitive Seat

*The horse loves a partner that gives distinct and understandable impulses and aids. The rider needs the feedback and confirmation from the horse.*

*Why are some riders relaxed on a horse and the horse moves harmoniously? Why do many riders have back pain after riding and the horse was unwilling and irritated? Why does the horse frequently not respond to the aids or misunderstands them?*

*To answer these questions, we need an individual and extensive evaluation of the rider on the horse. But, before analyzing how the rider moves when riding, we need to evaluate the posture at rest and correct it as needed.*

# BASIC ANATOMY

In order to understand the effect the rider's posture has on the horse and how the horse influences the rider, we must take a look at the anatomy of the human body. The basic anatomy of the upper body and the trunk are most important and are presented simply to make it easier to understand the complex processes in the body.

### The Vertebral Column

The vertebral column comprises seven neck, twelve chest, and five lumbar vertebrae as well as the sacrum and the coccyx. When seen from the side, the spine is shaped like a double "S." This shape serves as shock absorption under a load.

### The Vertebral Bodies

The vertebrae are connected to each other by muscles and tendons, are mobile at the vertebral junctions, and are separated by discs. The discs are made of a gelatinous core enclosed in an elastic fiber ring. They also have a shock-absorption function. With the "S" form of the spine, there is good mobility and an elastic spring action that protects the individual structures and enables an effective range of motion controlled by the muscles.

### The Rib Cage

The rib cage protects the internal organs such as heart, liver, spleen, and lungs. It is also important for breathing. It is composed of ribs that are attached to the thoracic vertebrae and in front at the sternum. This structure supports the thoracic spine. The lower ribs are not directly connected to the sternum, but to cartilage. When inhaling, the distance between the ribs increases and "the ribs are open." When exhaling the distance decreases and "the ribs are closed."

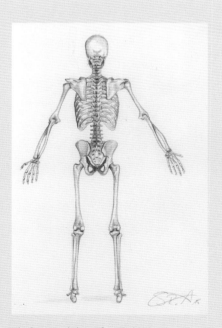

*The human skeleton from behind.*

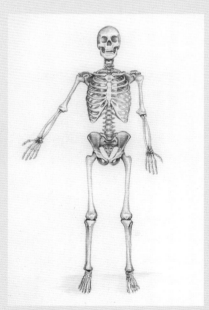

*From in front.*

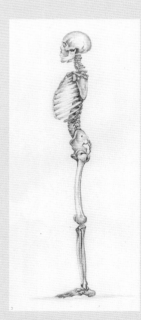

*From the side.*

### The Shoulder Girdle

The clavicle runs from the sternum to the shoulder blade and, thereby, connects the arms through the shoulder joints to the trunk with a great deal of mobility.

### The Pelvis

The pelvis comprises two hip bones that are attached to the sacrum behind, two seat bones, and the pubic bone. Both halves of the pelvis are connected together in front by strong connective tissue, the pubic symphysis.

### The Musculature

Muscles are responsible for all movement. Some are under our conscious control and directed by nerve signals. Some work unconsciously in circuits for posture control. Other types of muscles, such as heart and intestinal tract muscles, are not important for riding and are not discussed in this book.

Muscles can only contract and relax. Consequently, they work in pairs so that the previously contracted muscle can come back to the original length in order to contract again. For riding, at the shoulder, you need the chest muscles in front and the antagonist muscles that attach to the shoulder blade and pull back and down. On the upper arm, you need the muscles that raise and lower the arm. At the elbow and the wrist, you need the flexors and the extenders. In the trunk are the lengthwise, oblique and diagonal muscles of the back, side, and stomach. At the hip, we use joint extensors and flexors, muscles that turn the thigh in and out, as well as abductors and adductors. The muscles of the knee, ankle, and foot act similarly to the arm muscles.

### The Whole System

The system of components that carry the body and those that move the body is highly complex and requires the individual components to be perfectly in sync in order to be able to move at all. How the movement goes is dependent on the quality of the individual components, such as muscle mass, joint quality, or tendon and ligament stability, as well as the starting point of the movement.

The question to ask is: is there a specific posture where all actions (muscle tension, movement, relaxation, and return) are healthy, effective, and harmonious? Yes, it's erect posture.

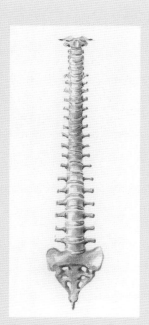

*The vertebral column from the front.*

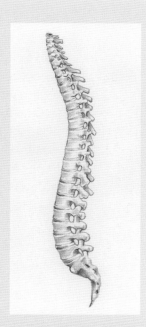

*The vertebral column from the side.*

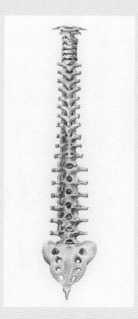

*The vertebral column from the back.*

*The skeletal musculature from the front.*

*The skeletal musculature from the back.*

# ERECT POSTURE

Erect posture is that posture where all the components of your vertebral column and the structures attached to it are in a relaxed position, from which movement in all directions is possible and to which it returns. We focus first of all on the posture of the head, trunk, and the pelvis in order to have a basic understanding about the posture of the upper body.

How should you think about erect posture? Your vertebral column should show the so-called double "S" shape to provide the advantages already discussed and to enable movement from a relaxed position. This also optimizes the horse's movements and leads to a harmonious and healthy coordination between rider and horse.

To keep it simple, the upper body is divided into three building blocks: head, chest, and pelvis. These are attached one on top of the other to make the double "S" shape.

- The "head" building block includes the skull and the neck vertebrae.

- The "chest" includes the vertebrae of the chest, the ribs, the sternum, the shoulder girdle, and the shoulder joints.

- The "pelvis" building block includes the lumbar vertebrae, the pelvis, and the hip joints.

When seen from the front and behind, the line of the shoulders should be parallel to the line of the pelvis. Both lines are parallel to the ground. Any deviation of any of the three building blocks, whether to the front, to the back, to the side, or rotation, disturbs your erect posture and leads to a bad starting position of the movement, which upsets your balance and results in an inharmonious interaction between rider and horse.

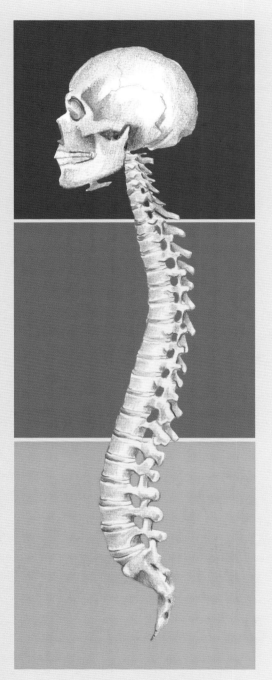

*The upper body (head and spine) as seen from the side divided into three building blocks: head, chest, and pelvis.*

# HOW DO YOU DEVELOP ERECT POSTURE?

*"Before approaching a horse, the student must understand her body position and the use of her arms and legs. Her body posture must put her in balance and show her the right way to use her limbs for guiding and grip. When she understands this on foot, she can get on a horse."*

*Die Reitkunst im Spiegel ihrer Meister* (The art of riding as seen through its masters) by Bertold Schirg (Olms Verlag, 1987)

The following practical exercise describes step by step how to develop erect posture. Practice statically—not on the horse. Control of this posture on a horse or in dynamic movement requires a longer period of practice.

**Standing Exercise**

- Stand sideways in front of a large mirror so that you can visually check and observe every step.

- Place your feet parallel and a little wider apart than your shoulders with knees slightly bent. This corresponds to the sitting position on a horse.

- Place your hands on the sides of your pelvis and move it forward and back without moving the rest of your body. For this selective pelvis tilt, imagine that your pelvis is a bowl filled with water, and dump the water out forward and backward.

- Find the middle position where the water in the imaginary bowl is level. That is the neutral position of the pelvis, from which you can move forward or backward, and to which the pelvis returns again. This is the primary movement in riding. The pelvis connects you to the movement of the horse.

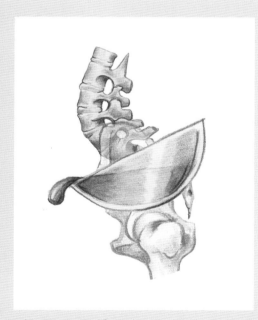

*Pelvis (water) tipped forward.*

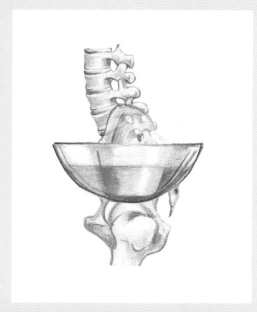

*Horizontal water level: neutral position of the pelvis.*

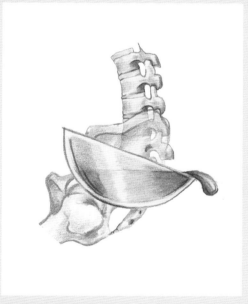

*Pelvis (water) tipped back.*

- Lift the sternum diagonally forward and up. Imagine that your sternum is pulled diagonally forward and up by a string.

- Put your hands on the sides of your rib cage and breathe deeply in and out to feel the movement of the ribs. With a deep exhale, the ribs close and the position is held by the tension of the upper abdominal muscles and the sternum is pulled as much as possible diagonally forward and up. In this way you are essentially breathing over the stomach (diaphragm) into the sides of the chest and the back area of the ribs (the back). The middle building block is held "plumb" and remains exactly above the pelvis building block.

- Let your arms hang loosely beside your body with the shoulder joints in a relaxed neutral position and the shoulder blades pulled down. Imagine that you want to stick your shoulder blades in your back pockets. From the side, your shoulder girdle should now be directly above the pelvis without being behind it. There should not be any rotation in your body.

- Straighten your head by taking the chin back a little (a slight double chin). The head is now in a neutral position between tending forward and backward. The neck vertebrae as well as the vertebrae of the chest are stretched upward while still maintaining their physiological curvature.

You are now in "erect posture." All of your movements come from this position. The component parts return to this neutral position after all movement. This posture enables the greatest possible mobility in all directions. An additional advantage is that your muscles aren't in a shortened position before a movement. This enables the rider to move optimally and to tense or relax with intention.

If you are in a bad position to start with, you will reach the endpoint of your motion quickly. The movement isn't smooth and incorrect loading creates tension with possible damage to discs and joints. Since it is also unpleasant for the horse when the rider is tense, he is resistant.

Riding consists of a constant exchange of impulses and signals from both parties. Habitual posture errors and deviations from an erect posture must be analyzed and can be corrected with appropriate and usually simple measures.

First we observe movement forward and backward and orient ourselves on a two-dimensional plane. Our body functions during movement with much more complexity. The concept of the three building blocks can now be used for a simple explanation.

*"Erect posture": neutral position.*

# INCORRECT POSTURES AND HOW TO CORRECT THEM

You now know how to think about correct—meaning erect—posture, theoretically. Analysis of individual problems and incorrect postures are imperative. Only when you know your weaknesses and posture errors can you avoid them and straighten up. The following examples can help you to analyze your posture yourself and correct typical posture errors. I recommend you get the help of experts with the analysis.

### Vulture Neck
When the head building block is positioned forward, we call this a "vulture neck."

*Correction point is the chin:* Bring the chin back a little (a slight double chin) to bring yourself into erect posture. Make sure that you don't take the chin back too far ("clamped neck"). Make sure the head building block is directly above the chest building block, and maintain the physiological curvature of the spine.

### Clamped Neck
When the head building block is too far back, we commonly speak of a "clamped neck."

*Correction point is the chin:* Bring the chin slightly forward to get back into erect posture. Avoid an overcorrection.

### Overstretching the Chest Vertebral Column
When the chest building block is positioned too far forward, we speak of an "overstretched chest vertebral column."

*Correction point is the ribs:* Close the ribs by exhaling and hold this position with muscle tension. Lay your hands on the sides of your ribs and breathe deeply in and out to feel the movement of the ribs. When exhaling deeply, the ribs close and the position is held by the tension of the upper abdominal muscles. The sternum should be pulled as much as possible diagonally up and out. You are now breathing above the stomach (diaphragm), into the sides of the chest and the back.

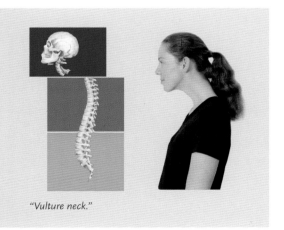
*"Vulture neck."*

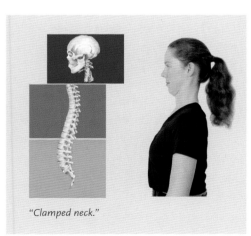
*"Clamped neck."*

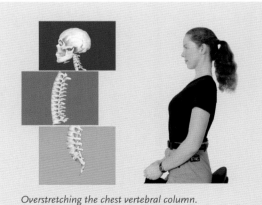
*Overstretching the chest vertebral column.*

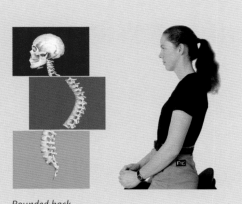

*Rounded back.*

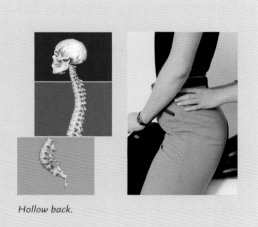

*Hollow back.*

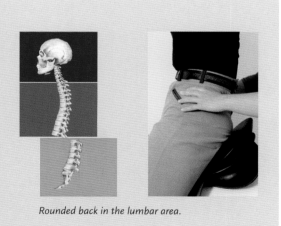

*Rounded back in the lumbar area.*

The middle building block is held "plumb" and is directly above the pelvis building block.

Make sure that you don't close the ribs too much ("rounded back"). Make sure the chest building block stays directly above the pelvis building block, and maintain the physiological curvature of the spine.

### Rounded Back

When the chest building block is thrust backward, we speak of a "rounded back."

*Correction point is the sternum:* Lift your sternum diagonally up and out. Be sure not to lift the sternum too much (overstretching the chest vertebral column), but make sure that the chest building block stays directly above the pelvis building block, and preserve the physiological curvature of the spine. The shoulder blades should be pulled back and down.

### Hollow Back

When the pelvis building block is thrust forward, the pelvis tips forward and we speak of a "hollow back."

*Two correction possibilities:* You can correct from the pubic bone by taking the pubic bone upward toward the sternum (bringing the sternum and pubic bone closer). Or you can correct from the image of the water bowl, with the pelvis tipped backward so that the water is running out the back (see p. 87). Both concepts lead to a neutral position of the pelvis and erect posture. Make sure that the tipping movement is not overdone or you will "round the back in the lumbar spine." Just get to a neutral position. Maintain the physiological curvature of the vertebral column.

### Rounded Back in the Lumbar Area

When the pelvis building block is thrust backward, we speak of a "rounded back in the lumbar spine."

*Two correction possibilities:* You can work either from the pubic bone correction point by moving the pubic bone away from the sternum, or you can imagine that the water bowl in the pelvis is dumping water out the front (see p. 87). Both lead to a neutral position of the pelvis and an erect posture. Make sure that the tipping movement is not done too much or you will end up with an over-extension in the lumbar spine (hollow back). Just come back to neutral position. Once again, the physiological curvature of the spine must be maintained.

Note:
*Knowledge about posture errors and their correction is only one component of improving posture. There are certain physical requirements that are necessary to bring theory to reality.*

# PHYSICAL REQUIREMENTS

Now that you have learned what erect posture is, and how to get it through correction points, it is very important to constantly strive and practice to make erect posture a habit. Naturally this is all connected with certain physical requirements, which are: mobility, stability, coordination, and body perception.

## Mobility

Mobility is required to get into erect posture and to get in sync with the movements of the horse. Mobility of the whole vertebral column, the hip joints, the chest, and the shoulders can be improved as necessary with targeted stretch and mobility exercises.

The mobility of one region is heavily influenced by the mobility of the neighboring regions. For example, movement of the pelvis automatically requires movement of the lumbar spine and the hip joints. Restriction in the hip joints affects the tip mechanism of the pelvis and, thereby, also the mobility of the lumbar spine. Restriction of the neck vertebrae influences the entire shoulder girdle.

*Note:* Without the mobility necessary for riding, movements are distorted and there is no harmonious movement pattern. Verify that you already have the necessary mobility or whether there is need for improvement. You can determine this, for example, with videos or photos.

## Stability

Stability is necessary for maintaining erect posture. Posture weaknesses and errors can be corrected by targeted strengthening of specific muscle groups. For example, powerful abdominal muscles compensate for the tendency to hollow the back. Powerful back muscles compensate for rounding the back. The lateral trunk muscles center the back, and the pelvic floor muscles stabilize the pelvis and trunk from within. The inner leg muscles (adductors) provide a stable seat and are, likewise, important for signaling the horse.

*Note:* Without the necessary ability to stabilize yourself for riding, movements won't be smooth, you will get tired quickly, and there will be no harmonious pattern of motion. Check to see if you have too much muscle tone, or, perhaps, your muscles are too weak. Some muscles need a lot of strength to create movement and others stabilize joints or the trunk.

## Coordination

Coordination refers to the ability to move the body by means of constant changes from muscle tension to relaxation, and the adjustment between mobility and stability—in every position of the body and in relation to the immediate environment, for example, when on a horse. Coordination can be improved through targeted practice of the same movement pattern in various types of sport and, ideally, also with music. Since riding is a rhythmically repeated series of movements, dance is particularly helpful. The most important coordinated capabilities of the body in riding are: a sense of balance, the ability to balance, spatial orientation, the ability to react, the ability to anticipate, and dexterity.

*Note:* If you aren't able to coordinate your own body, you will not have optimal control over a movement series. This makes it very difficult to give correct signals to a horse.

## Body Perception

Perception is the most important requirement for erect posture, because it gives you
the information about the present position of
your body and whether or not a correction is
necessary. Recognizing incorrect posture is
the first step to improving it by using the factors of mobility, stability, and coordination.

Body perception helps you to maintain
erect posture. In the beginning, you can practice in front of a mirror. Determine deficiencies and use the correction points as already
described. After practicing in front of the mirror, the visual check will be replaced by an
improved inner feel for your body. It is helpful
to have regular checks by partners, teachers,
physiotherapists, or video and photo analy-
ses. It would be ideal for you and also your
horse to practice while standing first, and
then taking the posture you have learned to
the horse. An example of an exercise for the
improvement of your body perception can be
found under the section "Perception" in the
chapter, "Practical Exercises" (p. 134).

*Note:* Without good self-perception, you can't
recognize and improve errors. Only a good
deal of self-criticism, as well as consciously
fixing your own body, can make you into a
good rider and enable a dialog with the horse.

*All four components should be in
harmonious balance and equally developed.
When one requirement is missing, the
pattern of movement is distorted.*

# IDEAL SEAT POSTURE AND RIDER MOVEMENT—BY GAIT

Basically, the rider's body should be in erect posture in all gaits, and only the pelvis should follow the movement of the horse.

*Halt:* The neck is long, the chin is slightly back, the shoulder blades are pulled down and back, the elbows are slightly bent and alongside the upper body, the sternum is lifted, and the ribs are closed. The pelvis is in a middle or neutral position out of which movement begins and back to which it ends. The distance of movement is the same forward and backward. All three building blocks are stacked one on top of the other.

The knees are slightly bent; the feet should be under the upper body in a horizontal position. As seen from the front and from behind, the shoulder line is parallel to the line of the pelvis. Both lines are parallel to the ground.

*Walk:* When the horse moves forward, the pelvis makes a tip and return movement with a small rotational component (three-dimensional movement). The rest of the body should remain quiet and stay in erect posture.

*Posting Trot:* It is important that the legs push down vertically on the stirrup when posting. This keeps the lower leg quiet and underneath you. Movement occurs only from the knees. As the horse pushes diagonally forward, the rider should straighten the upper body so that the diagonal push of the horse is allowed to pass through. That means that the upper body, while maintaining erect posture, is taken slightly forward when standing up. When sitting down the upper body should be vertical again.

*Sitting Trot:* At the trot the pelvis should rhythmically follow the movement of the horse. This also helps to reduce shock to the vertebral column. The rest of the body should stay quiet and in erect posture. As with all the other gaits, this requires precise muscle control and activity.

*Canter:* The movement of the pelvis is of great importance and follows the movement of the horse. The rest of the body should stay quiet and remain in erect posture. The movement of the pelvis is dependent on the size of the canter strides you want and can directly influence them.

*Stepping Over/Travers/Half-Pass/Leg-Yield:* A rotation of the whole body, not just the shoulders, is important. The rotation must be done synchronously and to the same degree by the pelvis and the rib cage. In this way, the whole body turns in one direction and the rotation also correctly affects the legs. The rotation is always in the direction the horse is moving. The rider's shoulders are always aligned with those of the horse. The rider's weight should be greater in the direction toward which the horse is moving. For example, when the horse is moving to the right, the weight is slightly more on the right. Your shoulder and pelvis lines should stay parallel to each other and to the ground. All the building blocks remain one on top of the other regardless if seen from the front or the side.

Unfortunately, a single error in posture within the building-block system affects the whole body and leads to negative compensation mechanisms that are hard to get rid of.

*Erect posture in the saddle.*

*Erect posture from behind.*

# THE MOST FREQUENT POSTURE ERRORS AND THEIR CONSEQUENCES FOR RIDER AND HORSE

The pelvis plays a central role. It is the connection point between rider and horse. Posture errors that have to do with the seat and the position of the pelvis are very common, but can be analyzed well— and ultimately, corrected. In addition, there are innumerable other posture errors or causes, as well as mixed patterns, that depend on the individual's anatomy, body type, personality, or emotional state. In this book, I can only touch on these points. There are many different reflexive reactions of the body and various compensation mechanisms. Every body can react differently to posture errors. On the pages that follow, I will describe the most frequent reaction patterns and compensation mechanisms.

## The Overextended Seat

In order to have an impression and an understanding of the descriptions and explanations that follow, I recommend a practical exercise for you to try at the same time as you are reading. Sit on the front third of a chair and put your upper body in erect posture. Now move your lumbar spine in an extreme exaggerated hollow back, meaning, tip the water out of the water bowl to the front (p. 87). Notice how your body reacts. In most cases, the following happens: the tip movement of the pelvis to the front and the resulting movement of the pelvis building block forward affects the chest building block reflexively. This is also moved forward and is in an overextended position. The shoulder girdle now moves behind the pelvis building block. The head building block is reflexively taken back, which causes a clamped neck.

This demonstration alone shows that a tiny change in posture—in this case,

the overextended lumbar spine—causes a chain reaction of several compensation mechanisms.

## What Happens at the Halt?

The lumbar spine is in a hollow-back position that tips the pelvis to the front. The spine of the chest responds likewise by overextending. The sternum is pulled up and the ribs are "open."

Because the sternum is lifted up and the ribs are now open, the shoulder girdle tips back, and is no longer above the pelvis building block when seen from the side, but behind it. Since the rider would fall forward due to the overextension, she tries to compensate by lying back in this overextended position. The leaning back also affects the position of her legs as described below. The chin is reflexively pulled back when there is an overextension of the chest vertebral column. The shoulder blades are shoved together and pressed down. The arms and the elbows are pulled to the body.

The hip joints are strongly flexed due to the forward tip of the pelvis. Normally, there is also an outer rotation and an abduction action in the hip joint. Because the rider is leaning back and the shoulder girdle is behind the pelvis, the rider must clamp the thighs on in order to not fall back, which is an active adduction. The knee joints are usually overflexed, the thigh is taken forward and up, and the lower leg is taken back in compensation.

Depending on the length of the stirrups, the feet are stretched down, or the toes are pulled up. This posture makes the rider's whole trunk musculature tense.

Now let's go back to a quiet sitting position. What happens in a dynamic process such as riding where every movement of the horse affects the rider?

## What Happens in Motion?

In dynamic movement, small errors in posture are magnified and cause much greater balance issues than in the static state (standing).

*Walk:* With the "push" from the horse due to his movement forward, the upper body tends to lean back. Just as when taking off on a motorcycle or in a car, you are thrown back. The rider tries to balance by shoving the chin forward.

*Posting Trot:* Taking the shoulders back tends to bring the whole upper body back. This intensifies the dynamic of the horse. To bal-

ance, the legs are taken forward. Pushing the legs down at the posting trot is no longer possible because they are directed forward. This then makes it impossible to take the upper body forward, which is important for keeping with the horse's movement. Typically, you know this process is happening when the seat plops down in the saddle. The legs have to be strongly clamped on to hold yourself on the horse, in this case. The flow of movement is jerky and cramped, and the horse feels disturbed in his back.

*Sitting Trot:* When the chin is shoved forward, the front neck musculature is at the end point of its movement span, which means it can't actively work anymore. The result is an unstable head posture with a nodding movement like a "bobble-head doll." The abdominal muscles are also not active and the ribs stay open; the upper body whips back and forth in a wave shape. This puts the lumbar spine as far as it will go in an even stronger hollow-back position. There is no longer any shock absorption. Discs and vertebral joints can be damaged and irritated, and the rider can feel pain.

*Canter:* The upper body leans back due to the strong forward push of the horse at the canter. A strong movement of the trunk compensates to take the body forward. This causes the rider to rock back and forth on the horse, which creates more problems. With the strong use of the upper body, the saddle is usually shoved from back to front. This is not desirable. The legs are strongly clamped on, which gives the horse the impression that you want an even stronger push forward. The rider often starts to pull back on the reins with the swing of the upper body, which signals the horse to go slower. This results in contradictory aids to the horse that necessarily leads to conflict. This same sequence often happens in the transi-

tion from walk to trot and from trot to canter (with any increase in tempo).

## The Rounded Seat

To better understand the description and explanation that follows, experiment with the following practical demonstration. Sit on the front third of a chair and put your body in erect posture. Exaggerate a rounded back, tipping the water backward out of the water bowl (p. 87). Now think about how your body reacts. In most cases, the following happens: tipping the pelvis backward pushes the pelvis building block backward, which reflexively works on the chest building block, which is also taken back, causing a rounded back. The shoulder girdle is now in front of the pelvis building block. The head building block must go forward, and this causes a "vulture neck."

## What Happens at the Halt?

The lumbar spine is rounded and the pelvis tips backward. The thoracic spine reacts by rounding, also. The sternum is drawn in and down. The abdominal musculature is inactive and slack. The shoulder girdle falls forward (protraction), the arms are rotated inward, the elbows point out and are too far away from the upper body. The shoulders are pulled up. The shoulder girdle is no longer above the pelvis building block, but in front of it. Since the rounded posture and the forward shoulder girdle would take the rider forward, she tries to equalize by leaning back in this posture, similar to how you see someone sitting on a Harley Davidson. Leaning back, likewise, affects the position of the legs. The chin is reflexively thrust forward when the back is rounded.

Tipping the pelvis backward extends the hip joint. Normally, this causes a reflexive

*The overextended seat.*

inward rotation (adduction) of the hip joint. Because the rider is leaning back, the thighs clamp on stronger to keep from tipping over. The knee joints are extended. The lower legs are shoved forward to counterbalance. Depending on the length of the stirrups, the feet are extended downward, or the toes are pulled up. You can't use your muscles in this posture. The seat is unstable.

*Walk:* With the push of the horse due to his movement forward, the upper body leans farther back, like it would on a motorcycle or in a car that has a jerky take-off and throws you back.

*Posting Trot:* Since the back is very round and leaning back, the legs are shoved forward and out with the rise of the post. The lower legs swing forward. This makes the rise impossible. The seat clamps together but can't rise out of the saddle. After this unnecessarily strong tension of the seat muscles, the body has to relax and the rider drops into the saddle. An active rise and sit is not possible. As the legs are shoved forward, the upper body is pushed back more, and the arms compensate by stretching forward. If the compensation doesn't work, the rider pulls hard on the reins. This causes the horse to move more slowly, which is seen as resistance.

*Sitting Trot:* Lacking the required abdominal and back tension, the upper body is unstable and rounds more against the force of the horse's steps. This leads to one-sided pressure on the front of the discs of the vertebrae and can cause damage (spondylosis and osteochondrosis of the chest vertebrae). The inactive neck musculature of the rounded-back posture allows the head to nod like a bobble-head doll.

*Canter:* Due to inactive musculature and the lack of effective control over muscle tension, the rounded seat has a strong effect on the whole body. The center of gravity of the body is too far back. With every stride, the rider is thrown farther back and moves like a pendulum forward in compensation. This is not a quiet picture. The effects on rider and horse are ultimately the same as with the overextended seat despite different posture errors (p. 96). The rider can stay on the horse only by locking on with the legs.

*The rounded seat.*

## The "Hollow-Round" Back

This is a combination of an overextended seat and a rounded seat and is recognized in an overextension of the lumbar (hollow back) and increased rounding of the chest vertebral column. This is very common and is merely called "bad posture."

The effects of the hollow-round back on riding are analogous to the consequences of riding with a hollow back and a rounded back. There are various combinations with localized deficits at other spots, according to the anatomical characteristics and the level of training of the rider. There can be movement limitations caused by injury to the shoulder and hip joints, stiffening of sections of the spine, neurological symptoms, and muscle cramping, all requiring careful analysis. Correction can be difficult and take a long time.

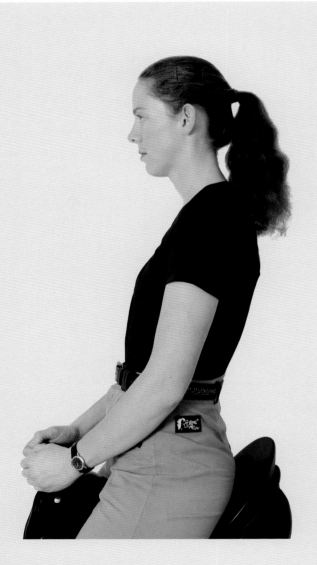

*The hollow-round back.*

### In a Nutshell

- A "small" posture error while standing still is worse in movement. Worst of all is how it affects the rest of the body when riding the horse.

- Well-trained horses react with sensitivity to the rider. Poor posture can cause contradictory signals, distorting responses and the normal flow of movement. A rider with a deficient seat cannot improve a poorly trained horse. The blame is not on the horse, but on the seat and posture of the rider.

- Only when the rider is in an erect posture, can she give the horse logical aids, and receive and send back impulses from the horse with sensitivity. From an erect posture, you can gently moderate a horse's deviations from correct movement, and actively correct him with soft pressure.

# Summary of the Most Frequent Errors Caused by Poor Posture or Poorly Used Muscles

*Walk:* Too much rotational movement due to insufficient musculature and lack of body control, especially in the shoulder region.

*Posting Trot:* The most frequent errors are pushing the legs forward or back instead of down. Usually the upper body is too far back, and the diagonal push of the horse is not maximized as already described. Unfortunately, this usually results in pulling on the reins and in contradictory aids to the horse.

*Sitting Trot:* The body is often unstable due to insufficient muscle tension. The rhythmic swing of the pelvis with the horse is not possible because the lumbar spine is stuck in an end position either with a hollow back or a rounded back. This results in abnormal loading of various structures, such as the discs.

*Canter:* Usually there is an excessive pendulum movement of the upper body that results in a "wiping" of the saddle. The upper body is not stable and is thrown out of control forward and back. The rider has difficulty staying on the horse and tries to compensate with legs clamped on.

*Stepping Over/Travers/Half-Pass/Leg-Yield:* Usually the body is over-rotated, so it can't work out of the center any more. This puts various muscles under a lot of tension, making it difficult to do movement patterns other than the rotation. Most riders mistakenly rotate only in the region of the chest. This is one of the biggest errors. The rotation must be synchronous and equal in the chest as well as the pelvis. This causes the whole body to turn in one direction. The rotation also puts the legs in the right place.

As you have learned, the seat should be slightly to the side in the direction of the movement of the horse. The most frequent error is misalignment of the parallel lines of the shoulders and pelvis. This is often seen as a collapse at the waist.

An additional error is pushing the chest building block out of alignment with the pelvis building block. The building blocks should always be one on top of the other, as seen from behind or in front.

*Shoulder and pelvis lines are out of alignment and there is collapsing at the waist.*

*Chest building block and pelvis building block are out of alignment.*

# THE SADDLE

The saddle is the location of the connection between rider and horse. You can find saddles of all sizes, shapes, materials, prices, and uses on the market.

The agony of having so many choices! The basics for selecting a saddle are:

- The saddle should have a supporting function and not force a rider into a certain position.

- It should do you and your horse "good," meaning it should allow an erect posture for you so that you can communicate through the saddle to your horse: you send signals and receive answers from your horse.

There are a couple of points regarding erect posture that you should keep in mind when choosing a correct saddle:

- There should be freedom of movement possible without restriction, but not *too much* space in which to move because that influences posture. Movement of the pelvis in all directions should be possible, however.

- There should be freedom of your legs with minimal support from blocks on the saddle (see p. 50). The thigh, in particular, must be free to take up an optimal leg position and to press on the right places on the horse in order to give aids.

- It needs well-balanced flocking for seat comfort and relief of the joints. It should provide support for the rider without being "spongy" or excessively soft.

- The saddle shape should not force the rider into a specific position.

- The rider's legs should hang down with slight flexion at the hip and knee, and with your feet horizontal resting softly on the stirrups— without your leg pressing against a block.

So how do you choose the correct saddle when you want erect posture? It is best to test various saddles, evaluate them according to

the following criteria, and ask yourself these questions:

**Position of the Pelvis**

Is there sufficient room for your pelvis to move? For example, can the pelvis tip forward and backward? Is it easy to find the pelvis' middle position (neutral)? When the saddle is tipped forward/downward, you will be forced into a hollow back, and a saddle that falls backward, meaning that it is too high in front, causes your pelvis to tip backward and forces you into a rounded back. This is what happens when the rider doesn't sit in the center of gravity of the saddle:

- Too far back and she will be forced into a hollow back.

*Saddle tips forward.*

*Saddle slopes back with the front too high.*

*Room for the pelvis: tipped forward, backward, and the neutral position.*

- Too far forward and the pelvis will tip back, resulting in a rounded back.

## Leg Position

Does the shape of the saddle at the thigh allow enough freedom of movement for aids to be given? Or does it force the thigh into a stuck or incorrect position? Are the stirrups attached too far forward or too far back?

Adjust the stirrups for the ideal length because the position of the thigh and lower leg is critical for the seat. When the stirrup is too short and forward, the thigh moves up and forward, and forms an angle of about 80 degrees in the hip joint, causing a backward tip of the pelvis into a rounded back. When the stirrup is too short and set on too far back, the thigh hangs down and back. This acts like a lever on the pelvis in the other direction, causing a hollow back. When the stirrup is too long and attached too far forward, a rounded back posture results, and positioned back and too long, a hollow-back posture is the result.

## Foot Position

When a stirrup is too short and the leg position is correct, the ankle is forced to bend too much; the heel is pressed down and the toe is lifted.

When the leg position is correct and the stirrup too long, the ball of the foot is pressed down and the foot is extended in a pointed-toe position.

*The saddle is not just a lovely place to sit. Any deviation from what is ideal for the individual has a direct effect on the contact surface of the seat and the whole body posture. Erect posture can only be achieved when a saddle is perfectly adjusted to the rider. With an erect posture, you can get in sync with the horse's movements and give the horse logical aids. The saddle is, therefore, the most important point of connection between rider and horse.*

*Blocks are too large causing an outward rotation of the legs.*

*Stirrups are too short.*

*Stirrups are too long.*

# PRACTICAL **EXERCISES**

*"Whoever doesn't want to devalue to the level of a trade this beautiful art that has been held in high honor since the dawn of history, and which should continue to be honored as long as courage and equestrian sense can be found in the human race, that person should engage first in training his own body and all parts of it to be supple and mobile, so that stiff arms and legs don't put improved understanding and feeling in chains..."* —Gustav Steinbrecht

*Die Reitkunst im Spiegel ihrer Meister* (The art of riding as seen through its masters) by Bertold Schirg (Olms Verlag, 1987)

The following chapter provides various exercises that can improve your physical ability and help you correct posture errors. An analysis of individual weaknesses and deficiencies in advance is necessary. Not every exercise is reasonable or productive for everyone. A physiotherapist should do the analysis. Some exercises are compensation training to relieve overused muscles and to counteract muscular imbalances. Other exercises are important to raise the level of muscle tone and, with it, the ability to stay in "erect posture" so as to enable a stable seat on the horse.

## Introduction

- All exercises must begin from an erect posture.

- You can make corrections using "Corrections, Tips, and Common Mistakes."

- Avoid compensatory and evasive movements.

- Every exercise program must be designed for the individual.

- The number, frequency, and intensity of exercises or the frequency of training sessions must be individualized.

- Age, general fitness level, constitution, and body type should be considered, and definitely be assessed by an expert.

- All exercises should be done after a basic physical warm-up.

- Please don't do any exercises without first consulting a trained expert.

# MOBILITY

## Exercises for Stretching Various Muscles

*For All Stretches:*

If burning or tingling occurs during a stretch, stop the stretch immediately. There are many types of stretch techniques—for example, static stretches and dynamic stretches. Which stretch technique is the best option for an individual should be discussed with a physiotherapist.

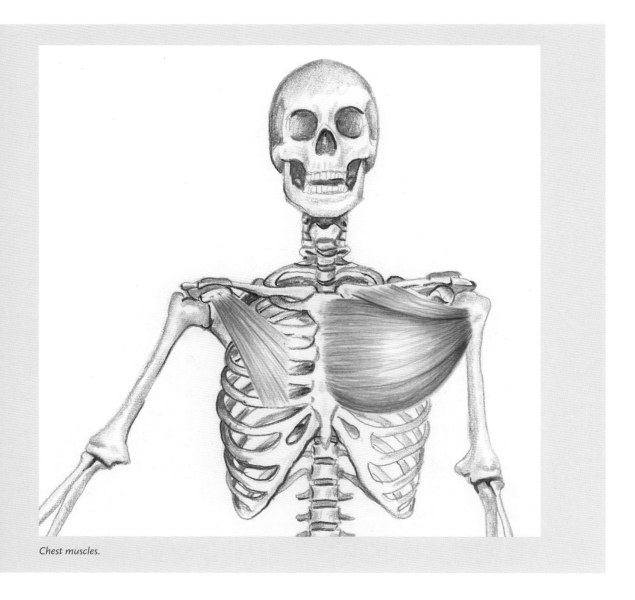

*Chest muscles.*

## Stretching the Chest Muscles

### Anatomy

There is a small (M. pectoralis minor) and a large (M. pectoralis major) chest muscle. The large chest muscle has three parts with different functions: the upper, middle, and lower sections.

The large chest muscle has the following functions:
- The whole muscle brings your arm to you and is responsible for rotation inward.
- The upper and middle segments move the arm forward.
- When the shoulder girdle is fixed the muscle aids respiration.

The small chest muscle is responsible for:
- Pulling the shoulder blades forward and taking the arms back when they are lifted more than 90 degrees.
- Assisting in breathing.

### Exercise Description

This exercise can be practiced in various positions. Depending on which region of the muscle is shortened, the stretch should be done in a 90-degree, greater than 90-degree, or less than 90-degree position.

*Starting Position:*
- Stand with your feet parallel and about hip-width apart.
- Bend your knees slightly and get in an erect posture.
- Put your lower arm on a door frame and in a position where the upper arm is parallel to the floor (90 degrees).
- Fix the shoulder blade back and down.

*Stretching to the End Position:*
- Move your body away from the arm that is to be stretched.
- Your feet must turn with your body so that there is no rotation in the spine.
- You should feel a pull in the middle region of the chest muscle.
- Stretch the muscle.

*Corrections, Tips, and Common Mistakes:*
- Make sure your upper body is in erect posture: No hollowed back (pull the navel in) and no rotation of the spine (place your feet in the direction of the movement).
- Make sure that your shoulder blades are pulled back and down. No raised shoulders.

*Variation 1:*
- Move to a position where the upper arm is below the shoulder joint (less than 90 degrees), so that the upper fibers of the chest muscle are stretched.

*Variation 2:*
- Move to a position where the upper arm is above the shoulder joint (greater than 90 degrees), so that the lower fibers of the chest muscle are stretched.

*Start position.*

*End position.*

*Variation 1: Start position less than 90 degrees.*

*Variation 2: Start position greater than 90 degrees.*

## Stretching the Shoulder Girdle Muscles

### Anatomy

The musculature of the shoulder girdle includes many muscles. In the following exercises, you will focus on only the trapezius muscle *(M. trapezius)* and the shoulder-blade lifter *(M. levator scapulae)*. The trapezius muscle comprises three sections: an upper, middle, and lower section.

Both muscles have an effect on the shoulder blade and on the spine of the neck. An optimal stretch of these muscles allows the extension of the spine in a physiological way so that the shoulder blades find their correct position back and down.

The trapezius muscle has the following functions:

- The whole muscle attaches the shoulder blade to the rib cage (thorax).
- The upper section pulls the shoulder blade diagonally upward and turns to the outside, tilts the head to the same side (ipsilateral) and turns it to the other side (contralateral).
- The middle section anchors the shoulder blade to the midline of the body.
- The lower segment pulls the shoulder blade down and toward the midline of the body.

The shoulder-blade elevator:

- Pulls the shoulder blade up and toward the midline of the body and
- Tilts the head to the ipsilateral (same) side.

### Stretching the Trapezius Muscle

*Start Position:*
This exercise can be done either standing or sitting.

*Standing:*

- Place your feet parallel to each other and about hip-width apart.
- Bend your knees slightly and get into an erect posture.

*Sitting:*

- Possible sitting positions: tailor's seat (a cross-legged position with the lower part of both legs folded toward the body, crossing each other at the ankle or calf, with both ankles on the floor), sitting on your heels, sitting on a chair or stool, or on an exercise ball.

*Stretching to the End Position:*

- Tilt your head down (chin to chest).
- Tilt your head away from one side.
- Now turn your head to the other side.
- Pull the shoulder blade down on the same side in the direction to which the head is turned.
- Stretch your muscles.

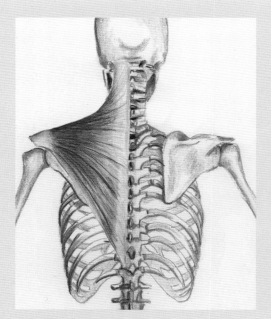
*Trapezius muscle.*

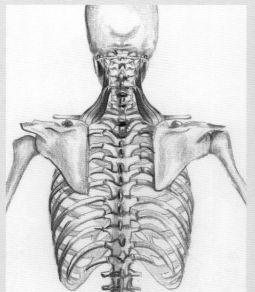
*Shoulder-blade elevator.*

*Stretching the trapezius muscle.*

*Corrections, Tips, and Common Mistakes:*
- Make sure that both shoulder blades are pulled back and down. No raised shoulders.
- Imagine that you are carrying a heavy purse on the side to be stretched so that your arm and shoulder are pulled farther down.
- The turning and tilting to the side happens only in the neck. Don't move other sections of the spine

### Stretching the Shoulder-Blade Elevators

*Start Position:*
This exercise can be done standing or sitting.
*Standing:*
- Place your feet parallel about hip-width apart.
- Slightly bend your knees and get into an erect posture.
- Pull both shoulders down and back.

*Sitting:*
- Possible sitting positions: tailor's seat; sitting on your heels; sitting on a chair, stool, or an exercise ball.

*Stretching to the End Position:*
- Tilt your head down (chin to chest).
- Tilt your head to one side.
- Now turn your head away from the side you are stretching.
- Pull the shoulder blade down hard on the side you are looking away from.
- Now stretch your muscles.

*Corrections, Tips, and Common Mistakes:*
- Make sure that both shoulder blades are pulled back and down. No raised shoulders.
- Imagine you are carrying a heavy bag on the side you are stretching so that your arm and shoulder are pulled farther down.
- The turning and tilting to the side happens only in the neck. Avoid moving any other section of the spine.

## Stretching the Hip Flexor

### Anatomy
The most powerful hip flexor is the *M. iliopsoas* and comprises two parts, the *M. psoas major* and the *M. iliacus.*

The function of this muscle is:
- Flexing and outer rotation of the hip joint.
- Lumbar spine: one sided contraction—lateral flexion to the ipsilateral side (flexion and turning outward on the same side); contraction on both sides at the same time—making the trunk erect from the back.

### Exercise Description

*Start Position:*
- Get on all fours.
- Take one leg forward and stretch the other leg far back.
- Straighten up your upper body and support yourself with your hands on your thighs.

*Stretching the shoulder-blade elevators.*

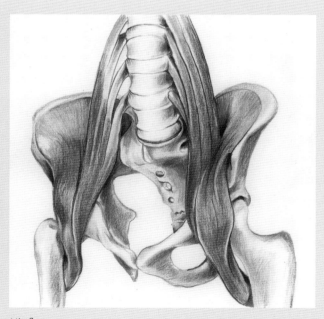

*Hip flexors.*

*Stretching to the End Position:*

- Bring your upper body into an erect posture.
- Lower your pelvis toward the floor.
- Tip the pelvis backward and make the groin long.
- Now stretch your muscles.

*Corrections, Tips, and Common Mistakes:*

- Keep the back knee straight.
- Make sure that neither leg is rotated. They must stay parallel through the whole exercise.
- You must actively tip the pelvis backward to avoid an evasive movement of the pelvis forward. You do this by tensing the abdominal muscles and pulling the pubic bone toward the sternum.
- Keep the angle of the front knee at least 90 degrees.
- Don't turn your upper body.

*Variation:*

- Put the knee of the back leg on the floor.
- Make sure that your pelvis is pushed forward and diagonally down, since the angle compared to the variation with the extended leg has changed.

## Stretching the Buttocks Muscles

### Anatomy

There are several muscles of the buttocks. They extend the hip joint and take the leg back, and include hip and buttock muscles. Here are a few examples of the outer hip muscles:

- *M. gluteus maximus*
- *M. gluteus medius*
- *M. gluteus minimus*
- *M. piriformis*

The functions of the buttocks muscles are:

- *M. gluteus maximus:* The whole muscle—extension and outward rotation of the hip joint; stabilization of the hip joint in the sagittal as well as in the frontal plane; cranial (upper) fibers—abduction (taking the leg away from the body); caudal (lower) fibers—adduction (bringing the leg toward the body).
- *M. gluteus medius:* The whole muscle—abduction, stabilization of the pelvis in the frontal plane; front portion—flexion and rotation inward; hind section—extension and outward rotation.
- *M. gluteus minimus:* The whole muscle—abduction, stabilization of the pelvis in the frontal plane; front portion—flexion and inward rotation; hind section—extension and rotation outward.
- *M. piriformis:* Rotation outward; abduction and extension in the hip joint; stabilization of the hip joint.

*Stretching the hip flexors.*

*Variation.*

**Description of the Exercise**

*Start Position:*
- Lie on your back and put both feet flat on the floor.
- Keep your upper body straight.
- Cross one leg over the other.
- The ankle should be over the thigh.

*Stretching to the End Position:*
- Grab the thigh of the leg that is still on the floor with both hands.
- Pull that leg toward your upper body.
- Stretch your muscles.

*Corrections, Tips, and Common Mistakes:*
- Avoid tilting your head back in the neck by taking your chin slightly back.
- Don't allow any twist in the spine and stay in an erect posture.

- Make sure that your ankle that is crossed over the leg can hang free so that there isn't pressure on the ankle.
- Your whole back should be in contact with the floor. Don't round your lumbar spine or the stretch effect will be less.

*Variation:*
- To strengthen the stretch, take your leg to the contralateral side (other side).
- Make sure that your whole back is still in contact with the floor.

## Stretching the Front of the Thigh

**Anatomy**

The front thigh muscle originates at the pelvis and on the thigh, and attaches below the knee joint. Consequently, this muscle affects the pelvis and knee positions. You must watch for this when stretching this muscle. The four-headed *M. quadriceps femoris* is part of the muscles of the front of the thigh.

The function of the front thigh muscle:
- *M. quadriceps femori:* consists of the *M. rectus femoris, M. vastus medialis, M. vastus lateralis,* and the *M. vastus intermedius.* It flexes the hip joint and extends the knee.

*Stretching the butt musculature.*

*Stretching the butt musculature—alternate view.*

*Variation.*

**Description of the Exercise**

*Start Position:*
- Lie on your side.
- Bend the legs in a 90-degree angle forward.
- Extend your arm upward and use it as a pillow.
- Keep your body straight.

*Stretching to the End Position:*
- Grab the top leg by the ankle.
- Pull the leg back and shove your heel toward your butt.
- Tip the pelvis actively backward to lengthen the groin.
- Now stretch your muscles.

*Corrections, Tips, and Common Mistakes:*
- Make sure the top leg is not twisted! It must stay parallel to the floor throughout the exercise.

- Actively pull your pubic bone toward your sternum to prevent your pelvis from going back with your leg.
- Make sure the bottom leg is in at least a 90-degree angle to keep you from hollowing your back.
- Don't turn your upper body.
- Pull your knee backward.

## Stretching the Back of the Thigh

**Anatomy**

The muscles on the back of the thigh originate on the pelvis and femur, and attach below the knee joint. Consequently, these muscles affect the position of the pelvis as well as the knee. This must be kept in mind when stretching these muscles. The muscles of the back of the thigh include the *M. biceps femoris*, *M. semimembranosus*, and also the *M. semitendinosus*.

The function of the muscles of the back of the thigh:
- *M. biceps femoris:* Opens the hip joint; stabilizes the pelvis in the sagittal plane; flexes the knee joint; and rotates the leg outward.
- *M. semimembranosus:* Opens the hip joint; stabilizes the pelvis in the sagittal plane; flexes the knee joint; and rotates the leg inward.
- *M. semitendinosus:* Opens the hip joint; stabilizes the pelvis in the sagittal plane; bends the knee; and rotates the leg inward.

**Description of the Exercise**

*Variation 1 Start Position:*
- Sit with your legs extended out in front of you and straighten the knee joints.
- Pull the feet up (toes toward your nose).
- Straighten your body.

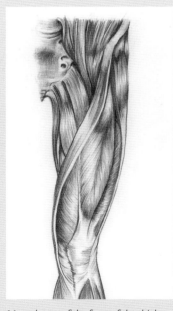
*Musculature of the front of the thigh.*

*Stretching the front of the thigh.*

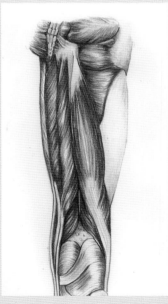
*Musculature of the back of the thigh.*

*Stretching to the End Position:*
- Straighten your upper body and tip forward toward your toes.
- Now stretch your muscles.

*Corrections, Tips, and Common Mistakes:*
- Avoid rounding your lower back.
- Keep the knees straight and the feet pulled up.
- Keep the legs parallel.

*Variation 2 Start Position:*
- Lie on your back and put both feet on the floor.
- Make sure your upper body is straight.
- Stretch one leg toward the ceiling.

*Stretching to the End Position:*
- Put your hands around the thigh of the leg that is stretched toward the ceiling.
- Straighten the knee joint.
- Pull the foot toward your nose.
- Pull the leg toward your upper body.
- Stretch your muscles.

*Corrections, Tips, and Common Mistakes:*
- Avoid bending your neck backward by pulling your chin back.
- Your whole back should be in contact with the floor; don't round the lumbar spine (lower back) because that weakens the effect of the stretch.
- The leg must be pulled parallel to the body with no rotation or tipping toward the outside or inside.

## Stretching the Inside of the Thigh (Adductors)

### Anatomy
Adductors pull the thigh toward the body. There are adductors that don't run over the knee joint (see the exercise with bent knees, p. 112) and there is an adductor in the hip joint that does go over the knee joint (see the exercise with straight knees p. 112).

The function of the adductors:
- The adductors that originate on the pelvis and attach to the femur function mostly as adductors and outward rotators of the hip joint. Most adductors also stabilize the pelvis in the frontal and sagittal planes. Some of these muscles also flex the hip joint. The adductor that attaches below the knee affects two joints: it bends and adducts both the hip joint and the knee (flexion and inward rotation).

*Variation 1: Stretching the back of the thigh sitting with outstretched legs.*

*Variation 2: Stretching the back of the thigh lying on the back.*

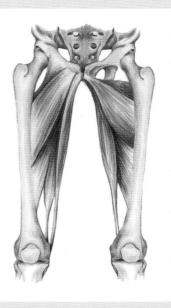

*Adductor muscles.*

**Description: Stretching the Adductors That *Don't* Run Over the Knee Joint**

*Start Position:*
- Sit on the floor with the soles of your feet touching.
- Let the knees fall to the outside.
- Keep your upper body straight.

*Stretching to the End Position:*
- Grab your ankles with your hands.
- Actively push both knees toward the ground.
- Now stretch your muscles.

*Corrections, Tips, and Common Mistakes:*
- Keep your back straight and avoid rounding or over-extending (hollowing) your lumbar spine (lower back).

*Variation 1:*
- Place your hands on your knees on the same side and press down.
- At the same time, turn your upper body toward the other side and support yourself with a hand on the floor.
- Don't let one side of your butt lift off the floor.

*Variation 2:*
- With a straight back, lean forward.
- Grab your ankles with your hands.
- Put your forearms on your lower legs and press down.

**Description: Stretching the Adductors That *Do* Run Over the Knee Joint**

*Start Position:*
- Sit on the floor with your legs spread.
- Keep your back straight.
- Pull your feet up (toes toward your hip joints).

*Stretching to the End Position:*
- Straighten your knee joints.
- Stretch your muscles.

*Corrections, Tips, and Common Mistakes:*
- Keep your back straight and make sure you don't round or hollow your lumbar spine (lower back).

*Variation/ Increasing the Stretch:*
- Keeping your back straight, lean forward.
- Support yourself with your hands on the floor in front of you.

*Stretching the adductors that **don't** run over the knee.*

*Stretching the adductors that **do** run over the knee joint.*

## Stretching the Calf

### Anatomy

*M. triceps surae* is the main muscle of the calf. This muscle is divided into the *M. gastrocnemius* (two-headed muscle) and the *M. soleus*. Since the *M. gastrocnemius* is a two-joint muscle, it affects both the ankle and the knee joints. This should be kept in mind when stretching this muscle.

The function of the calf muscle:
- The whole muscle: movement of the foot (foot taken down); supination and inversion of the foot (lifting of the inside edge of the foot).
- *M. gastrocnemius:* bending the knee.

### Description of the Exercise

*Start Position:*
- Stand up straight.
- Place your feet parallel about hip-width apart.
- Bend your knees slightly.
- Take a big step forward with one leg.

*Stretching to the End Position:*
- Bend the front leg slightly.
- Extend the back leg.
- Actively push the heel to the floor.
- Stretch the muscles.

*Corrections, Tips, and Common Errors:*
- Don't rotate or tip your pelvis.
- Don't rotate your legs but keep them parallel.

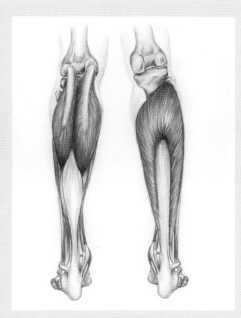

*Left: M. gastrocnemius. Right: M. soleus.*

*Stretching the calf.*

## Exercises for Isolated Movement of the Spine

These exercises teach your body to isolate, coordinate, and control specific regions of the body. This is especially important for making corrections, because you must learn how to do individual actions like "close the ribs" without moving and rounding the whole spine, for example. In the following exercises all directions of movement are included to encourage optimal mobility in all directions.

*Moving the pelvis forward.*      *Middle (neutral) position.*      *Moving the pelvis backward.*

In the following exercises, make sure that you move only that part of the body that you are exercising. Prevent movement in other regions of the body. Move from one end of the exercise span to the other quietly and fluidly without any jerks.

## Moving the Pelvis Forward and Backward

*Start Position:*
- Stand up straight.
- Place your feet parallel about hip-width apart.
- Bend your knees slightly.

*Doing the Exercise/End Position:*
- With your hands on either side of the pelvis, move your pelvis forward and backward without moving the rest of your body (selective tipping of the pelvis).

- Imagine your pelvis is that bucket full of water and that you are pouring water out the front, then out the back.

*Corrections, Tips, and Common Errors:*
- Keep your back straight.
- Keep the knees slightly bent.
- Only move your pelvis.

*Variation:*
- You can also do this exercise sitting on a chair or stool, an exercise ball, or even on a horse.

## Moving the Pelvis Right and Left

*Start Position:*
- Stand up straight.
- Place your feet parallel about hip-width apart.
- Slightly bend your knees.

*Doing the Exercise/End Position:*
- Place both hands on the sides of the pelvis, and move it to the right and to the left by first lifting one hip and then the other.

*Corrections, Tips, Common Mistakes:*
- See "Moving the Pelvis Forward and Backward" on this page.

*Moving the pelvis to the right.*

*Moving the pelvis to the left.*

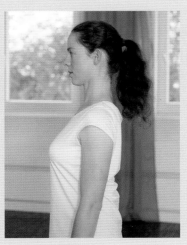

*Move the rib cage forward (lift the sternum).*

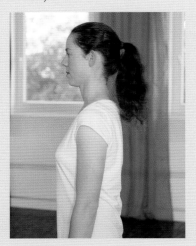

*Middle (neutral) position.*

*Move the rib cage backward (sink the sternum).*

## Moving the Rib Cage Forward and Back

*Start Position:*
- Stand up straight.
- Place your feet parallel about hip-width apart.

*Doing the Exercise/End Position:*
- Move your rib cage forward and back by lifting your sternum diagonally forward and up, then take it back and down.

*Corrections, Tips, and Common Mistakes:*
- Keep standing up straight.
- Keep the knees slightly bent.
- Move only as described above.

*Variation:*
- You can also practice these movements sitting on a stool or chair, on an exercise ball or on a horse.

## Moving the Rib Cage to the Right and Left

*Start Position:*
- Stand up straight.
- Place your feet parallel about hip-width apart.

*Doing the Exercise/End Position:*
- Move your rib cage in the horizontal plane to the right and to the left.
- Imagine once again the building-block system and move the whole rib-cage building block to the right and left.

*Corrections, Tips, Common Mistakes, and Variations:*
- See "Move the Rib Cage Forward and Backward," above.

*Move the rib cage to the right.*

*Middle (neutral) position.*

*Move the rib cage to the left.*

*Moving the head forward.*

*Middle (neutral) position.*

*Moving the head back.*

## Moving the Head Forward and Backward

*Start Position:*
- Stand up straight.
- Place your feet parallel about hip-width apart.
- Slightly bend your knees.

*Doing the Exercise/End Position:*
- Move your head forward and backward by taking your chin forward and backward on a horizontal plane.

*Corrections, Tips, and Common Mistakes:*
- Make sure you stay standing straight.
- Keep the knees slightly bent.
- Only move your head as described above.

*Variation:*
- You can also do this exercise sitting on a chair or stool, an exercise ball, or on a horse.

## Moving the Head to the Right and Left

*Start Position:*
- Stand up straight.
- Place your feet parallel about hip-width apart.
- Bend your knees slightly.

*Doing the Exercise/End Position:*
- Move your head to the right and left in the horizontal plane.
- Imagine the building-block system and move the whole-head building block to the right and left.

*Corrections, Tips, Common Mistakes, and Variations:*
- See "Moving the Head Forward and Backward" on this page.

## Exercises for Mobilizing and Stretching the Whole Spine

The spine is capable of moving in all directions: rotation, lateral bend, forward bend, and stretching up. It is, therefore, a very mobile system. Mobility of the spine is especially important for riding since the rider must be in sync with the movements of the horse and must go with him. This can be practiced and improved upon with several mobilization exercises. It also requires a certain amount of mobility to be in erect posture. This is only possible if there is optimal mobility of all the sections of the spine. For example, when the spine of the chest is restricted, you can't straighten it, which keeps you from getting into an erect posture.

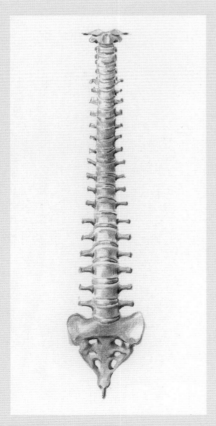

*The spine from the front.*

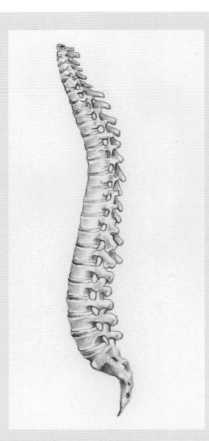

*The spine from the side.*

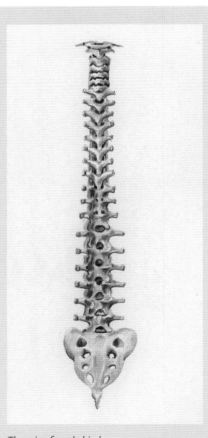

*The spine from behind.*

## Turn-Stretch Position/ Mobilization in Rotation

*Tip: This exercise can also be used to stretch the chest muscles.*

*Start Position:*
- Lie on your back and place both feet on the floor.
- Keep your upper body straight.

*Doing the Exercise/End Position:*
- Place your hands to the right and left of your body on the floor in a U-position (90-degree bend of the elbows and 90-degree abduction of the arms).
- Lift your knees up and take them to the floor on one side.
- Let your head lie on the floor turned in the opposite direction.

*Corrections, Tips, and Common Mistakes:*
- Don't hollow your back.
- Your arms should be in contact with the floor throughout the stretch.
- If you can't reach the floor with your knees, put a pillow under them so that your knees can relax. Having to hold them will have a negative effect on the stretch.

*Variation:*
- Do the exercise with crossed legs.
- Make sure that the leg that is over the other one touches the floor to increase the tip to the side.

## Standing on All Fours/Mobilization of the Spine in Bend and Extension

*Start Position:*
- Get on all fours.
- Have your arms vertical directly beneath your shoulder joints and your legs under your hip joints. You should have a 90-degree angle in both joints.
- Slightly bend your elbows.
- Bend your knees 90 degrees.
- Place your lower legs and the back of your feet on the floor.
- Keep your back straight.
- Pay attention to the position of your head. The chin should be in a soft, double-chin position and the neck vertebrae should be an extension of the spine of the rib cage.

*Turn-stretch position with knees lying against one another.*

*Turn-stretch position with crossed knees.*

*Arching the back.*

*Middle (neutral) position.*

*Sway back.*

*Doing the Exercise/End Position:*

- Arching the back: From the start position, round your back by pulling all the sections of the spine into a rounded position. Take your head down, pull the sternum in, close the ribs, move the spine of the rib cage toward the ceiling, pull your navel toward your spine, and tense your abdomen. Lift your pubic bone toward your sternum, which will tip your pelvis back (water bucket dumps out behind) and tighten your butt muscles.
- Start position/middle position: return to the starting position and straighten your back.
- Sway back: this is an overextension of the spine. Pull the spine into an over-extended position: lift the head up, pull the sternum toward the floor, open your ribs, move the rib cage toward the floor, let your navel sink toward the floor, and relax your abdominal muscles. Take your pubic bone away from the sternum, which will tip your pelvis forward (water bucket spills out the front). Push your butt upward. The lumbar spine is now hollowed.

*Variation:*
- If being on all fours is uncomfortable in the hand and elbow joints, you can do these exercises supported on your forearms.
- If pressure from the mat causes pain in your knees, you can put a pillow under them.

*Corrections, Tips, and Common Mistakes:*
- Move only as described—up and down without rotation or sideways movement.
- Make sure your start position is correct.
- This exercise also helps train your perception of erect posture.

## Standing: Mobilizing the Spine Sideways

*Start Position:*
- Stand up straight.
- Open your legs parallel and about shoulder-width apart.
- Bend your knees.

*Doing the Exercise/End Position:*
- Slowly tip your upper body to the right and to the left, and hold to the side.
- Always hold a moment in the middle.
- Imagine that you are between two walls (one in front and one behind you).
- Stabilize your pelvis.

- The movement should occur only above the pelvis.

*Corrections, Tips, and Common Mistakes:*
- Make sure there is no other movement, especially no rotation, bending forward, or over-extending the spine.
- Keep your pelvis fixed and don't pull it up when leaning to the side.

*Variation:*
- To increase the lean to the side, your arm can be taken up and over in the direction to which you are leaning. When leaning to the left, your right arm is taken up and stretched.

*Mobility is not only important in dancing, but also in riding.*

# STABILITY

## Exercises for Strength and Stabilization

*Strengthening the Abdominal Muscles*

Since you have many different abdominal muscles with various functions, I am giving you here a large assortment of exercises. Please analyze your body and your areas of weakness so that the exercises are effective for your body, and they help you—as an individual—to improve your posture.

**Anatomy**

Simply put, there are lateral, oblique, and straight abdominal muscles. The muscles have different points of origin and attachment and, consequently, have different jobs and functions. The *M. obliquus externus abdominis, M. obliquus internus abdominis,* and the *M. transversus abdominis* are lateral, oblique abdominal muscles. The *M. rectus abdominis* is a straight muscle of the front abdominal wall. Since attachments are also on the pelvis, the abdominal musculature affects the movement of the trunk, breathing, and also the pelvis. This must be kept in mind during the exercises. The abdominal musculature can be trained for movement of the pelvis and also to create a lever effect on the legs. In particular, these exercises train the lower segments of the abdominal musculature.

The function of the abdominals:

- *M. obliquus externus abdominis:* unilateral—lateral flexion (leaning to the side) of the trunk on the ipsilateral (same) side; rotation of the trunk to the contralateral (opposite) side; bilateral— forward bend of the trunk, lifting of the pelvis, crunches, and exhaling.
- *M. obliquus internus abdominis:* unilateral—lateral flexion of the trunk to the ipsilateral (same) side; rotation of the trunk to the ipsilateral side; bilateral— bend of the trunk forward, lifting of the pelvis, crunches, and exhaling.
- *M. transversus abdominis:* unilateral— rotation of the trunk to the ipsilateral side; bilateral—stomach crunches and exhaling.
- *M. rectus abdominis:* bending the trunk forward, lifting the pelvis, stomach crunches, and exhaling.

## Exercise for Strengthening the Oblique Abdominal Muscles

*Start Position:*
- Lie on your back with both feet on the floor.
- Make sure your upper body is straight.
- Tip your pelvis backward and move your lumbar spine toward the floor.
- Put both hands on the right and left sides of your head.
- Lift your head and shoulders a little from the floor.
- Bend both legs about 90 degrees in the knees and the hip joint.
- Pull your toes toward your nose.

*Doing the Exercise/End Position:*
- Move your diagonal knee and elbow together at the same time.
- Let the other leg sink softly toward the floor.
- Turn your upper body diagonally.

- A strong exhale increases the activity of the abdominal musculature during the exercise and affects the floor of the pelvis, as well. Exhaling increases the training effect.

*Corrections, Tips, and Common Mistakes:*
- All movements should be done with strength and not with force.
- You want a smooth and fluid change.
- Don't hold your breath but let it flow calmly and powerfully: a powerful exhale increases the training effect.
- Don't put your shoulders down on the floor but keep them in the air.
- Maintain a soft double chin.
- Keep your shoulders pulled back and down (away from your ears).

## Exercise for Strengthening the Lower Region of the Straight Abdominal Musculature

*Variations 1 Start Position:*
- Lie on your back and place both feet on the floor.
- Make sure your upper body is straight.
- Tip your pelvis backward and move your lumbar spine toward the floor.
- Bend both legs: about 90 degrees of bend in the knee joint, and about 90 degrees of bend in the hip joint.
- Pull your toes toward your nose.
- Move your knees toward your feet and stay in a position where the tension of the abdominal muscles increases markedly, but keep the lumbar spine on the floor (starting position).
- Lay your arms along the sides of your body.

*Strengthening the oblique abdominal muscles.*

*Variation 1 (Starting Position): strengthening the lower region of the straight abdominal musculature.*

*Variation 1 (Doing the Exercise/End Position): strengthening the lower region of the straight abdominal musclature.*

*Variation 2 (Doing the Exercise/End Position): strengthening the lower region of the straight abdominal musculature.*

*Doing the Exercise/End Position:*
- Move the soles of your feet one at a time away from you.
- While doing this, exhale powerfully but smoothly, which increases the activity of the abdominal musculature, and affects the floor of the pelvis, as well. Exhaling increases the training effect.

*Corrections, Tips, and Common Mistakes:*
- All movements should be done with strength but not with force.
- A fluid change is desirable.
- Don't hold your breath but breathe calmly and powerfully. A powerful exhale increases the strengthening effect.
- Don't move your knees more than described in the start position since that lessens the tension on the abdominal muscles and, therefore, lessens the training effect.

*Variation 2 Start Position:*
- Lie on your back and place both feet on the floor.
- Make sure your upper body is straight.
- Tip your pelvis back and move your lumbar spine toward the floor.
- Lift your legs toward the ceiling with a 90-degree bend in the hip joint; allow a slight bend in the knees.
- Pull your toes toward your nose.
- Lay your arms at your sides on the floor next to your body.

*Doing the Exercise/End Position:*
- Lift your butt up from the floor, then let it sink back down.
- Imagine that you are pulled toward the ceiling by the feet.
- A powerful but smooth exhale during the exercise increases the activity of the abdominal muscles, and also affects the floor of the pelvis. Exhaling increases the training effect.

*Corrections, Tips, and Common Mistakes:*
- All movement should be done with strength but not with force.
- Avoid moving your legs forward and back.
- It should be fluid.
- Don't hold your breath but breathe calmly and powerfully. A powerful exhale increases the strengthening effect.

## Exercise for Strengthening the Straight Abdominal Musculature

*Start Position:*
- Lie on your back and put both feet on the floor.
- Make sure your upper body is straight.
- Tip your pelvis backward and move your lumbar spine toward the floor.
- Lift your head and shoulders from the floor.
- Look in the direction of your knees.
- Lift both arms from the mat.

*Doing the Exercise/End Position:*
- Move your arms in small but quick and controlled movements up and down. The amount of movement is about 6 inches.
- The musculature is activated and strengthened by the quick, small movements of the arms.

*Corrections, Tips, and Common Mistakes:*
- Move the arms from the shoulders so that there is a lever effect with an increase in tension of the abdominal muscles.
- Avoid bending the elbows and wrists.
- Maintain a double-chin position and the direction of your eyes as described.
- Keep your shoulders pulled back and down.
- Don't hold your breath but let it flow calmly and powerfully. A powerful exhale increases the strengthening effect.

*Strengthening the straight abdominal musculature.*

## Strengthening the Back Muscles

Since you have many different back muscles with different functions, I am giving you a large number of exercises. Analyze your body in advance to determine your weak areas so that the exercises are effective for you, and you can improve your posture.

### Anatomy

Simply put, there is, on one hand, the autochthonous back musculature (innate and developmentally "old"). This consists of many different muscles grouped together as *M. erector spinae* and forms a deep layer of back muscles. On the other hand, there is the so-called secondary, evolved ("younger"), superficial back musculature. This includes, for example, the already described *M. levator scapulae* or the *M. trapezius*. Due to the various attachment and origin points as well as the different depths (deep, superficial), the muscles have different jobs and functions.

The function of the back muscles:

- Since naming all of the muscles would be too much, we will only describe the various functions of the whole back musculature. The functions of the *M. trapezius* and *M. levator scapulae* have already been explained elsewhere in this book (p. 106).
- *M. erector spinae:* Extension and stabilization of the individual segments of the spine through bilateral tension; leaning to the side and rotation of individual vertebral segments when tensed unilaterally.

The following exercises strengthen the whole back, the neck, as well as the muscles of the shoulder blades. To strengthen the back, a starting position where the muscles must work against weight (lying on your stomach, being on all fours) leads to an optimal and healthy training effect without using weights.

## Strengthening the Back Lying on Your Stomach

*Start Position:*

- Lie on your stomach.
- Make sure your upper body is straight.
- Tip your pelvis backward (dumping water out the back) and imagine you are pulling your navel toward your spine and away from the floor. The stomach muscles are now active and work against a hollow lumbar spine.
- Put your toes and the balls of your feet on the floor
- Straighten your knees.
- Lift your shoulders and head up.
- Lift your arms in a U-position (90-degree spread of the arms at the shoulder and 90-degree bend in the elbows).

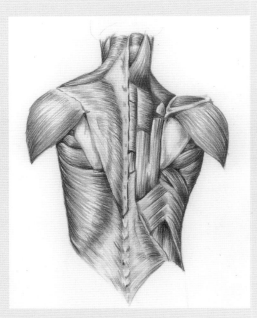

*Superficial back muscles.*

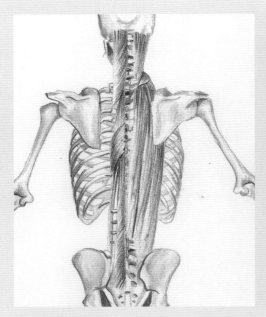

*M. erector spinae: deep back muscles.*

*Starting position.*

*Doing the Exercise/End Position:*

- Alternate the left and right arms, pushing them forward and backward.
- Pull the elbows toward the feet and extend the other arm forward.

*Corrections. Tips, and Common Mistakes:*

- Don't hollow your back, and keep your body straight throughout the exercise.
- Keep your shoulders down and back (away from your ears).
- Maintain a double chin so that you don't over-extend the cervical spine.
- Keep the forearms and elbows horizontal to the ground.

*Variation:*

- Extend both arms forward and up and lay the arms on the floor.
- Lift one arm and the diagonal leg alternating and hold this position.
- Don't hollow your back; keep your body straight during the whole exercise.
- Don't press away from the floor with the hand that is lying on the floor. Work with the strength of the back muscle.

*The end position.*

*Variation.*

## Back Strengthening Exercise from an All-Fours Position

*Start Position:*
- Get on all fours.
- Have your arms directly under your shoulder joints and your legs under your hip joints. You will have 90-degree angles in both joints.
- Slightly bend your elbows.
- Bend your knees 90 degrees.
- Have your lower legs and feet on the floor.
- Make sure your upper body is straight.
- Pay special attention to the position of your head. The chin should be in a soft double-chin position so that the neck vertebrae serve as an extension of the thoracic spine.

*Doing the Exercise/End Position:*
- Changing up diagonally, lift one leg and one arm and hold in this position.

*Corrections, Tips, and Common Mistakes:*
- Don't hollow your back; keep your body straight during the entire exercise.
- Hold your shoulders back and down (away from your ears).
- Keep a soft, double-chin position so that you avoid an over-extension of the neck vertebrae.
- Arms and legs should be parallel.
- Don't tip your pelvis or rotate the spine.

*Variation:*
- If being on all fours is uncomfortable for you in your wrists or elbows, all of the exercises can be done supported on your forearms.

## Strengthening the Butt Musculature

Training the butt muscles and the hip-joint extenders helps even out uneven muscle tone. Since most riders overuse the hip flexors, for example, by constantly pulling the legs up, training the antagonists (the opposite muscles) is logical to develop the same muscle tone in both muscle groups. Strengthening the seat muscles can be even more successful when it is done in combination with stretching the hip flexors (see Stretching Exercises, p. 107). The goal is to achieve the same harmonious muscle tone, strength, and suppleness in all muscle groups. This allows the rider to give reasonable and useful aids if her body can get in harmony with passive and active movements

**Anatomy**
See page 108.

*The starting position.*

*Doing the exercise/end position.*

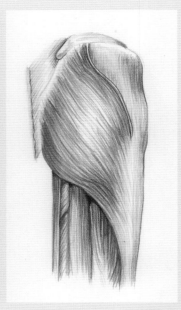

*Butt musculature.*

## Description of the Exercise

*Start Position:*

- Get on all fours.
- Have your arms directly under your shoulder joints and your legs under the hip joints so that you have 90-degree angles in both joints.
- Bend your elbows slightly.
- Have a 90-degree angle in your knee joints.
- Your lower legs and feet should be on the floor.
- Make sure your upper body is straight.
- Pay special attention to the position of your head. As said before, the chin should be in a slight double-chin position so that the neck vertebrae are an extension of the thoracic spine.

*Doing the Exercise/End Position:*

- Lift one leg backward.
- Maintain the 90-degree angle in the knee.
- Pull the toes of the lifted leg so that the foot is parallel to the floor.
- Move your thigh toward the ceiling until it is parallel to the floor.
- Then take your leg back to the starting position and repeat the movement.

*Corrections, Tips, and Common Mistakes:*

- Don't tip your pelvis or rotate the spine.
- Activate your abdominal muscles so you don't hollow your back.
- Keep your upper body straight during the whole exercise.
- Keep your shoulders down and back—away from your ears.
- Maintain a slight double-chin position to avoid overextending the neck.

*Variation:*

- Stay in the end position with the thigh parallel to the floor.
- Move your leg in small pushes, about 4 inches at the most, upward and downward.

*The starting position.*

*Doing the exercise/end position.*

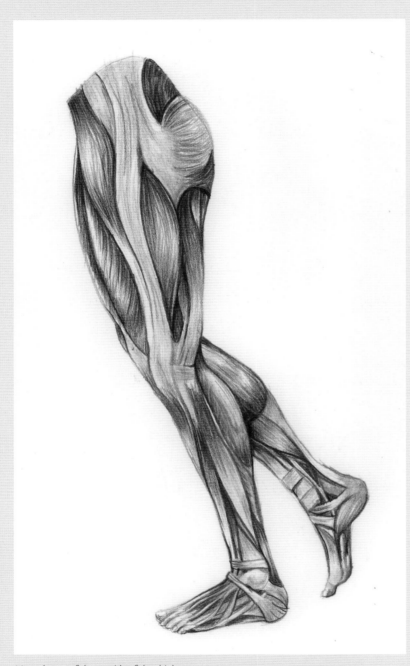

*Musculature of the outside of the thigh.*

## Strengthening the Outside of the Thigh

Training the outside of the thigh is important for evening out muscle tone. Since most riders overuse the inside thigh muscles, for example, when constantly clamping the legs, training the antagonists (the opposite muscles) is logical to develop even muscle tone in both muscle groups. Strengthening the outer-thigh muscles can be done in combination with stretching the adductors (see p. 111) for more benefit. The goal is to achieve the right muscle tone with the same power and suppleness in all muscles. This helps the rider to give logical and useful aids.

**Anatomy**

Most of the muscles of the outside of the thigh are abductors. They spread the hip joint and the legs, and involve hip and butt muscles, as well as thigh muscles. Here are a few examples of muscles that act as abductors:

- *M. gluteus maximus*
- *M. gluteus medius*
- *M. gluteus minimus*
- *M. tensor fasciae latae*
- *M. piriformis*
- *M. satorius*

The function of the muscles of the outside of the thigh:

- As with the butt muscles already described on page 108, the *M. tensor fasciae latae* and the *M. satorius* are also abductors.
- *M. tensor faciae latae:* tenses the fascia lata; abduction, flexion, and inward rotation of the hip joint.

- *M. satorius:* abduction, flexion, and rotation outward of the hip joint; flexion and inward rotation of the knee joint.

**Description of the Exercise**

*Starting Position:*
- Lie on your side.
- Keep your upper body straight.
- Support your head with one arm.
- The arm should be an extension of the trunk.
- Slightly bend the leg on the floor.
- Lift the upper leg and make sure that this is done in alignment with the trunk and that it doesn't move forward or backward.
- Pull your toes of the upper leg toward your nose.
- Straighten your knee.

*Doing the Exercise/End Position:*
- Lift your leg to the side about 45 degrees toward the ceiling, then lower it again to the starting position.
- Make sure the leg is only lifted from the side and not forward or backward, or in rotation.

*Corrections, Tips, and Common Mistakes:*
- Don't turn the leg by rotating the hip joint.
- Don't tip your pelvis or rotate the spine.
- Keep your body straight throughout the whole exercise.

The starting position.

Doing the exercise/end position.

## Whole-Body Strengthening Exercises

It is logical to train the whole body along with individual and targeted muscle groups. In such a complex sport as riding, individual muscle groups are seldom active—rather the whole body and multiple muscles are used.

### Strengthening Exercise Supported on the Forearms

*Start Position:*
- Lie on your stomach.
- Get on your toes.
- Straighten your knees.
- Tense the muscles of the butt, abdomen, and back.
- Pull your sternum diagonally forward and up.
- Drop your shoulder blades down and back.
- Shove your chin a little back (slight double chin).
- Place your forearms on the floor.
- Tense your entire body.

*Doing the Exercise/End Position:*
- Lift your body from the floor. Only the forearms and the balls of your feet/toes should have contact with the floor.
- Your body should be in a line from head to heel that reflects the anatomical form of the body: for example, double "S" shape of the spine, butt a little higher, a dip at the knees.

*Corrections, Tips, and Common Mistakes:*
- Keep your body straight; avoid hollowing the lumbar spine, rounding the back in the rib cage or over-extending the neck.
- Make sure the butt is not positioned too far up or down.

*Variation 1:*
Without losing the straightness in the upper body, move the body from this position forward and backward. Don't let the butt go up or down.

*Variation 2:*
Changing hands, support yourself on the hand and stay there a few seconds. Then go back to supporting yourself on the forearms. Avoid too much rotation in the body and keep your body straight.

### Strengthening Exercise from the Side

*Start Position:*
- Get on your side.
- Support yourself with your forearm on the floor.
- Straighten your knees.
- Pull your toes toward your nose.

*Doing the Exercise/End Position:*
- Lift your pelvis and straighten your body.
- The body is not in a diagonal position.

*Corrections, Tips, and Common Mistakes:*
- Don't let your upper body tip forward or backward.
- Keep your upper body straight.
- Keep your shoulder blades down and back.
- Don't let your pelvis drop, but also don't lift it too high.

*Variation:*
- Lift your leg to the side about 45 degrees toward the ceiling and then lower it again to the starting position. This strengthens the outside of the thigh and the hip-joint abductors.
- Make sure the leg is only lifted sideways and that there is no rotation of the hip joint.
- Make sure your pelvis doesn't sink toward the floor when you lift your leg.

*Forearm stance.*

*Side support.*

*Variation.*

# COORDINATION

To build body coordination, many of the exercises already described can be done on an exercise ball or a balance board. Being on something mobile imitates the movements of the horse and trains coordination of various body parts and muscle groups. It is also recommended for riders to engage in similar types of sport that ideally train coordinated capabilities, such as dancing. Wherever you live, you can probably participate in a group dance class or take individual instruction. Learning choreographed dances allows a transfer of coordination to the rhythmically moving horse.

# PERCEPTION

The special importance of this has already been mentioned. Checking in the mirror as you do the exercises I have provided is a wonderful way of visually training perception. The goal is to learn to feel posture mistakes without visual aid.

In the following example, perception of erect posture is trained. These steps help you to internalize and remember this posture. Please do Step 2 after you can do Step 1 without problems or mistakes. Repeat the individual steps multiple times in a day to develop body memory over time.

## Step 1: Basic Exercise

Stand sideways in front of a mirror (profile). Watch each movement carefully and quickly correct it using what you see in the mirror. It is also good to do these exercises in the presence of trained experts.

- Place your feet parallel and a little farther apart than your shoulders with knees slightly bent.
- Put your hands on your hips and move your pelvis forward and backward without moving the rest of your body (selective pelvis tilt). Imagine that your pelvis is a filled water bucket and that you are dumping the water out to the front and then to the back.
- Find the middle position where the water would have a horizontal level.
- Lift your sternum forward and up. Imagine that your sternum is pulled by a thread diagonally forward and up.
- Lay your hands on the side of your rib cage and breathe deeply in and out, and feel the movement of your ribs. With a deep exhale, the ribs close and the position is maintained by tensing the upper abdominal muscles. At the same time, the sternum should go as far as possible diagonally up and forward. You are breathing essentially over the diaphragm into the side of the rib cage and in the back of the ribs (the back).

- Let your arms hang loosely next to your body. The shoulder joints should be in a relaxed neutral position, and the shoulder blades pulled down. Imagine you want your shoulder blades in your back pants pockets. From the side, your shoulder girdle should directly be over the pelvis, neither forward nor behind. There should also be no rotation.
- Straighten up your head by pulling your chin slightly back (a slight double chin). The head is now in a neutral position between being forward and backward. The neck vertebral column is an extension of the chest vertebral column while still maintaining its physiological curvature.

## Step 2

Practice the exercise in Step 1. Now after each individual step, close your eyes and *feel*. Search for the feeling of the correct position and remember it.

## Step 3

Do the basic exercise again, but now close your eyes before each individual step. With closed eyes, try to find the correct position, and open them when you are in the correct posture for *you*. Now check your posture in the mirror and correct it, when necessary. If corrections are necessary, focus on them with closed eyes, and go on to the next step of the exercise.

## Step 4

During all the steps of the basic exercise, keep your eyes closed. Open your eyes after you have done all the steps of the exercise, and check your posture in the mirror. If corrections are necessary, focus on them with closed eyes, followed by checking again in the mirror.

## Veronika Brod and Her Work

Veronika Brod has loved horses since she was a child, like many of her friends. She enjoys riding most of all, but also enjoys other activities like cleaning stalls and caring for the horse. Since she was three years old, dancing became another passion—first classical ballet and later modern dance.

Riding and dance both involve rhythmic movement of the body. In both there is a musical dialog either with other dancers or with the horse as the riding partner.

After training to be a certified gymnastics instructor at the Bode School in Munich, Germany, she attended the internationally famous Iwanson—International School of Contemporary Dance—also in Munich.

Since 2008, she is the co-founder and owner of a dance school in Weilheim in Oberbayern, where special emphasis is placed on "healthy movement" in diverse forms of dance. Along with experience as a dance teacher, she also works daily in gymnastics and fitness, especially in her work as a physiotherapist.

Her personal experience and her love for horses, paired with knowledge about healthy body posture and movement, led her to focus on "rider and horse and how they can interact in a way that is healthy for both."

# POSTURE PUZZLES

In this section, you will have the opportunity to study the posture that the rider should be in for the various lateral movements. See if you can tell which lateral movement our model Silvia Wimmer is doing on the ground. You will also find many mistakes in body posture in the pictures. These can be very confusing for the horse because they confuse the aid. See if you can tell correct from incorrect positions!

You will find the answers to the Posture Puzzles on page 144.

## Incorrect Postures

In order to correct mistakes in body posture, it is important to recognize which mistake the rider is actively making, and which posture errors are merely chain reactions. For example, you can ask the question if the rider is collapsing in the hip and the shoulder line is crooked as a result, or if one shoulder is dropped that is causing the hip to collapse. Correction must focus on the primary error and the rider should try to develop the correct awareness.

# FIRST PUZZLE

*Which Movement?* The rider is looking away from the direction of the movement, the weight is slightly to the left, the right leg drives a little sideways while the left is kept slightly back guarding.

*Frequent Mistake:* The rider collapses in the right waist, the weight goes too much to the left, the right leg is taken up and back from the bent knee and the left leg is stiff.

Answer on page 144.

# SECOND PUZZLE

*Which Movement?* The rider is looking to the inside, the shoulders and the pelvis are likewise turned to the inside and are aligned. The left leg drives sideways and the right leg is guarding the hindquarters.

*Common Mistake:* The rider collapses to the left in the waist, the weight goes too much to the right, while the shoulders and pelvis are no longer parallel to the ground, but are lower on the left side.

*Common Mistake:* The rider leans to the left away from the direction of movement, the weight stays to the left, and she is pushing the horse away to the side, and the shoulders and pelvis are crooked.

Answer on page 144.

# THIRD PUZZLE

*Which Movement?* The rider is turned to the wall, and is looking in the direction of movement. The weight is a little to the left, the left leg is bent and at the girth and drives the horse forward, while the outside leg drives sideways.

*Common Mistake:* The rider collapses to the left, the weight goes to the right, the left leg is stiff and can no longer support bend and position well. Shoulders and pelvis are not in alignment.

*Common Mistake:* The rider's weight falls to the left while collapsing in the right waist. The left leg is stiff and shoulders and pelvis are not in alignment.

Answer on page 144.

# FOURTH PUZZLE

*Which Movement?* The rider is looking in the direction of movement with her weight slightly to the right. The left leg is taken a little back and drives sideways while the right leg holds the horse forward on the girth and supports bend and position.

*Common Mistake:* The rider is leaning in the direction of movement while collapsing in the right waist, which causes the right shoulder to drop. She is holding her head crooked and her upper body is a little behind the vertical.

*Common Mistake:* The rider is leaning with the upper body to the right, the right shoulder is too low, and she is holding her head crooked.

Answer on page 145.

# FIFTH PUZZLE

*Which Movement?* The shoulders are exactly over the pelvis and the head is held straight. The left leg is at the girth to drive the horse forward and to support bend and position, while the right leg brings the hindquarters along laterally. The weight goes slightly to the left.

*Common Mistake:* The rider collapses in the waist, the weight falls to the right, the lines of the shoulders and pelvis are no longer parallel to the floor.

*Common Mistake:* The rider turns the outside shoulder too far in the direction of movement. The pelvis is left behind so that shoulders and pelvis are no longer aligned, and the upper body is crooked.

Answer on page 145.

# SIXTH PUZZLE

*Which Movement?* The shoulders are above the pelvis and both lines run parallel to the ground. The inside leg is at the girth to maintain position, bend, and forward movement. The outside right leg moves the hindquarters sideways The rider is looking slightly to the left.

*Common Mistake:* The rider leans to the left, collapses at the waist, and is crooked.

*Common Mistake:* The rider takes the outside shoulder too far forward, gets crooked, and holds her head crooked.

*Common Mistake:* The rider collapses to the right, the right leg is too far back, she is looking too far to the left, and the shoulder and pelvis lines are no longer parallel.

Answer on page 145.

# POSTURE PUZZLE ANSWERS

### First Puzzle

Leg-yield: Vera Munderloh on the Lipizzaner stallion Maestoso Stornella

### Second Puzzle

The shoulder-in: The inside hind leg and the outside front leg are on the same track. The upper body is turned slightly toward the inside of the arena without collapsing and staying erect. Vera Munderloh on Favory Toscana.

### Third Puzzle

Travers: The horse is bent around the rider's left leg. She sits in the direction of movement with erect posture and relaxed shoulders and arms. Jana Lacey-Krone on Maestro.

## Fourth Puzzle

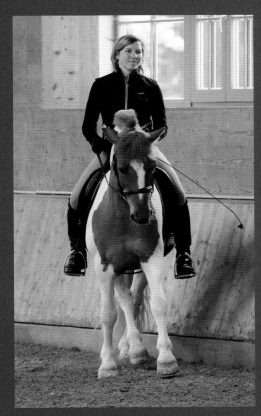

Renvers: The horse is bent and positioned in the direction of movement. The rider looks a little to the left and is stepping more in the left stirrup. The upper body is straight and the arms fall down loosely. Nadine Kloser on Chuck.

## Fifth Puzzle

Half-pass: Vera Munderloh on the Lipizzaner stallion Tulipan Palma.

## Sixth Puzzle

Half-pass: The rider goes with the horse with the weight slightly in the direction of movement without leaning to the side. Vera Munderloh on Alaraz.

# IN **CONCLUSION**

You can work on a good seat your entire life and always improve it. The results you are striving for will benefit you in your everyday life and influence your posture positively. It is worth the effort, not just for your horse, but also for you, to accept the challenge and constantly train, reflect, and improve your inner image in order to ultimately develop the best possible unity between body and spirit. The art of riding is not just an activity with a horse and an education in posture. It is also a school of life!

Anja Beran

# APPENDIX
## PREREQUISITES FOR LEARNING TO SIT WELL

Anyone fascinated by horses and wishing to learn the high art of riding wonders about how to best approach the subject. In the text that follows, I have prioritized, listed, and explained the many requirements.

### A Well-Trained Horse

For a young rider, a mature, experienced and well-trained horse is a basic requirement for learning a correct seat. Only a "straight" horse allows a rider to sit symmetrically. A relaxed, swinging back that "invites" the rider to sit is the foundation of instruction. Traditionally, we considered a school horse to be one that is highly trained. Such a horse is fantastic to teach beginning riders because he won't be dull or require too much of the student's energy to keep him going, nor will he run off and not allow her to sit. The contact will be quiet and even so that the rider learns from the beginning how careful she must be with her hands if she doesn't want to cause a harsh reaction from the horse. This horse will teach the student the concept of "rhythm" from the beginning. And he will react positively to every correctly given aid, providing the new rider with an "aha" experience. As technique and feel improve, the horse rewards the rider directly. On the other hand, such a horse won't react badly when the wrong aid is given. Consequently, a well-trained school horse is the most important "riding instructor" for a beginning rider because he delivers prompt and clear responses to what is done in the saddle. He gives the rider an extraordinarily fine feel.

If I let the student piaffe on a school horse now and then, the horse will give her the correct feeling in the seat, better than

*A good seat requires constant control and striving for improvement. Anja Beran on Campeao.*

what any riding instructor from the ground could ever say in words, because the piaffe positions the rider like no other exercise can. Naturally, such a horse must be ridden afterward by a trainer to keep him supple and sensitive. Otherwise, the student would soon make him dull to the aids and unbalanced, and the positive benefit of his training would be lost. Above all, I'm aware of horses that are insufficiently trained and, consequently, teach the student bad habits instead of helping her.

I avoid horses that are heavy, dull, on the forehand and hard in the mouth. They can ruin a beginner, because she will tend to be rough in the saddle, assuming that is "normal," and completely lose any sensitivity that should actually be taught in the riding art.

Despite the common notion, a horse that is merely well-behaved is not ideal for a beginner. If he hasn't been sufficiently trained through gymnastics and is, therefore, stiff, the riding student will never be able to sit with suppleness because he is hard in the back and tosses the student around. He will be dull to the calf and won't react to mistakes of the hand. Poorly or insufficiently trained horses are often resigned and simply accept the mistakes of the rider without objecting to them. It is impossible to learn on him. When the horse hasn't been trained well enough, the riding student might correctly give an aid, but the horse doesn't respond because he doesn't know the aid. This is frustrating for the student, the horse, and also the riding instructor standing in the arena.

The riding instructor and the horse should work as a team to educate the student in the high art of riding. This means that the trainer should be able to use a whip from the ground to teach certain exercises, for example, piaffe and passage, and the student only has to concentrate on following the movement and feeling the exercise. If the trainer is working with a horse-rider combination where both don't know what they are doing, success is very difficult to achieve, if at all.

The student doesn't have the opportunity to communicate in a simple language of the aids because she is too busy staying straight in the saddle and coordinating her body, as is the horse. He has no chance of finding his balance because the rider is constantly disturbing it. Moreover, he has to decipher "aids" out of uncoordinated signals being sent from the saddle to which he is somehow to react right or wrong. The future is very bleak for a horse that starts being treated like a poorly trained or worse yet, a problem horse. Horses without a solid foundation react to unpleasant riders according to their nature. Some become dull and resigned while others become nervous or defensive, because they simply don't understand what the rider wants from them. The saying, "Old rider/young horse and young rider/old horse," is true, but is rarely followed today.

A further significant advantage of an older, highly trained horse is not just physical ability, but also the psychological maturity of such an animal. Years of training have brought a high school horse to a level of maturity that gives him a high degree of trust in humans and also self-confidence. Such a horse will give the student a feeling of security and calm rather than fear of shying, sudden nervousness, or bolting. This is exactly what she needs to be able to concentrate on learning a good seat.

*My advice for all interested in learning the art of riding: keep an eye out for an appropriate school horse!*

Gustav Steinbrecht wrote that a well-trained school horse is of immeasurable value for teaching a rider the correct seat. He also said that no one should have her first experiences on a stiff, untrained horse. He wrote:

*"There is nothing more backward than to put a student on a crooked, complicated philistine of a horse and then to ask her to force herself into some semblance of a normal seat on this caricature of a riding horse, expecting that in this physical struggle she can achieve inspiration or riding feel. The old masters put their student on a fully trained school horse, even in the pillars, without stirrups and reins. In this way, the student was able to gradually sit down, make her seat broad, and let her legs hang down naturally, so that the ordered, rhythmical movement of the piaffe could bring her quickly into a feeling of being one with the horse....*

*"The student was next trained, likewise on a school horse, on the longe, and learned again without stirrups or reins the same thing in motion that she learned on the spot between the pillars, namely softly snuggling into all the movements of the horse, in other words, the BALANCE that results in a good and secure seat more than the highly touted tight grip of the legs. Trained in this way with the occasional soft reminders from the instructor, the student finds the beautiful form of the seat almost by herself, finds joy in riding, and develops for her whole life what is the most important thing in riding—sensitive rider feel.*

*"The young student who wants to be a professional rider should not begin in any other way. Today we hear the loud complaint that there aren't any riders any more to whom one can entrust a young horse without great worry. This is the natural consequence of there no longer being academic riding schools where people are trained on school horses that are the true teachers of the riding student."*

*The Gymnasium of the Horse* by Gustav Steinbrecht (Xenophon Press, 2014)

This passage by Gustav Steinbrecht is very important, because today we are clearly living with the dilemma he describes. There are so many people who are excited about horses and riding, but there is a distinct lack of excellent school horses to teach them. Deficiencies of the seat lead to rough aids and even end up with the rider discovering new training methods that are actually completely unnecessary if she simply knew about the thorough gymnastic training of a horse according to classical principles. Most riders today are not under pressure to earn a living with their horse, and their life doesn't depend on surviving a military battle—instead, they ride as a hobby. Happily, in more recent times, I sense a movement that is bringing more people to the classical way, which will be of great benefit to horses. At this time we should remember the great riding master Egon von Neindorff who said:

*"For the beginner, the best horse is exactly good enough."*

Die Reitkunst im Spiegel ihrer Meister (The art of riding as seen through its masters) by Bertold Schirg (Olms Verlag, 1987)

Many readers know that it is hard to have a well-trained school horse available. Such horses are hard to find and when you find one they are generally expensive. I know this problem well and am often frustrated by it. Consequently, I will focus on the *ideal* conditions for learning the art of riding, and that includes a perfect school horse.

## A Competent Riding Instructor

The search for a good riding instructor is a big job because they aren't on every corner. Take the time and energy to look broadly. Remember that a few good lessons accomplish more than a lot of bad ones. Ask to watch a lesson being taught and check to see how many good students the instructor has taught and which horses he has trained.

Only in this way can you be sure that you will be in good hands. Riding is a dangerous undertaking and you are entrusting your physical health to an instructor.

I am frightened by how carelessly things are done. The best protective riding gear doesn't help if the horse is not educated and the ride looks risky from the beginning.

The riding instructor of your choice should be an experienced trainer who ideally has also trained the horse you are learning on. He and the school horse must work well together to help you get started. This means the school horse should respond to the instructor's smallest aid, and they should trust each other. The rider should also have the feeling that the riding instructor can assess the horse and keep him under control. If this expectation is not met, the new rider might soon give up because she finds herself in an uncontrollable situation. Quiet competence and a large measure of sympathy are additional desirable characteristics in a riding instructor to help build trust with the student. In addition to his psychological sensitivity, the instructor's knowledge helps to reduce fear and anxiety in the student.

From the start, it is mandatory that the instructor teach the beginning rider to respect the horse, and show her over and over why it is important for the horse that the rider move in the saddle in this way or that, and that some actions are absolutely taboo— for example, balancing herself on the reins.

*The idea of good "behavior" in the saddle as it relates to the poor creature having to endure it should be taught from the first lesson on.*

Only in this way can a rider be educated to think about it, always question herself, and constantly try to get better. Consequently, don't go to an instructor that speaks disparagingly of your school horse or pushes you to handle him roughly. The tone of the environment in a riding school will tell you quickly whether this is a place where the art of riding is nurtured or it is a school of a lower level that is primarily commercial. In the latter case, you will not learn to develop a supple seat or how to give fine aids.

Since the riding instructor must influence the posture of the student above all, it is important that he work frequently with a physiotherapist: the instructor gains insight into how the human body moves and can give his student valuable advice. If the instructor is not trained in this way, any seat corrections he gives will be limited to merely technical commands about how the rider's posture should look, which might be very hard for the pupil to accomplish. It is very valuable to look at the development of the seat from another point of expertise. It helps the student understand the causes of her errors so she can fix them rather than just focus on them. For example, someone who is stuck in a "fork" seat might have weak abdominal muscles. The instructor should focus on these to help fix the problem.

Generally speaking, it is very important for the riding instructor to always watch the symmetry of the student. Are her shoulders at the same level? Is she collapsed at the waist or is one leg longer than the other? Such mistakes can make a correct seat on a horse very difficult and are also hard on the horse. Therefore, it is important for the riding instructor to explain the negative

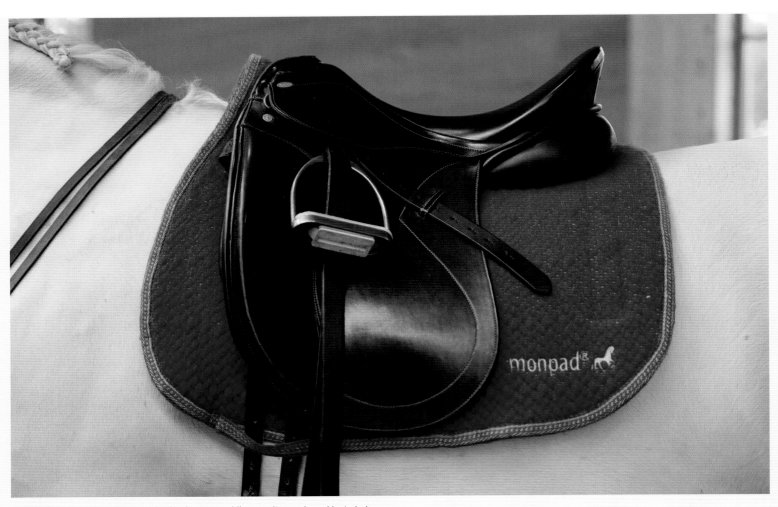

*For a rider to be able to sit correctly, the dressage saddle must lie evenly and be in balance.*

consequences of the student's seat and recommend she visits a physiotherapist. This can help with the development of physical balance and mobility and every rider should take advantage of cooperation between these two experts.

A non-riding physiotherapist comes to our barn regularly to watch the students. She helps us riding instructors by suggesting where the seat corrections need to be made. Physiotherapists can often see the cause of the problem while a riding instructor might be focused only on the symptoms. Moreover, they can give the students appropriate gymnastic exercises to practice at home to improve their physical capabilities.

## A Suitable Saddle

The saddle plays a vital role because it is the point of connection between the rider and the horse's back. When it is uncomfortable for the horse, his back tenses, and he won't let you sit well. If you feel uncomfortable or crooked, or if the saddle is too small, you won't be able to sit in a supple way, which again leads to the horse bracing. A good saddle fitter should have horse and rider in mind in order to establish an ideal starting point for a good seat.

Since I am discussing the classical dressage seat, which is the basis for all other ways of riding a horse, it is important to use an appropriate dressage saddle. A comfortable saddle will make your effort to find the correct posture while mounted on a horse considerably easier. Like a dance partner, it should guide you gently and relaxed into the right posture. It must have a correct center of gravity and fit the horse's back. All the effort to sit straight is for nothing when the saddle

*This saddle is not lying correctly—the center of gravity is too far back. The rider would feel like she is on a slide falling backward and won't be able to find her balance.*

*This saddle is tipping forward, which makes it impossible for the rider to sit in the center of gravity.*

shoves you forward or you slide crooked and backward. Lateral symmetry in the saddle must also be assured, because you can't sit in the middle of a saddle that is crooked and not evenly adjusted left and right. It is possible that it is not the fault of the saddle but instead the horse is not symmetrically muscled, which causes the saddle to be crooked. However, such a horse is not well trained and should not be a school horse for this reason.

The saddle should also fit the size of the rider. A small rider will slide around in a large saddle and find it difficult to get in the right spot because the side panels are too long and make it difficult for her to effectively use her legs. Likewise, a larger, heavier rider will feel restricted in a small saddle and won't be able to freely give aids.

*The saddle must, therefore, fit both horse and rider, and the rider must feel comfortable.*

Beginners often prefer saddles with very large knee rolls because they make them feel secure. You should keep in mind, however, that the seat is not secure and quiet because you can lock onto a knee roll, but rather because you are in balance—without restriction from knee rolls or blocks. A small block that gives support in an emergency yet serves as a soft guide to the leg is good, but a large, thick block permanently against the thigh restricts and limits free movement of the hips. Many riders complain about pain in the hips after a lesson in such a saddle. The saddle should be constructed so that the rider can have a comfortable seat that is "broad in the pelvis" with her legs hanging down loose instead of giving her only a small sitting surface and pressing against the thighs.

*Here, the stirrups are too short and will shove the knee up and forward away from the saddle. The calf muscle becomes tight and hard, and the rider will sit in a chair seat.*

*Stirrups that are too long put the rider on her tip toes and into a fork seat.*

*You can best find the ideal stirrup length by starting with a loose, hanging leg. You should be able to reach the stirrup by just lifting the toe.*

The placement of the stirrup bar is also important. When it is too far forward, the rider is forced into a chair seat, and when it is placed too far back, her thigh is pulled too far back and she will fall into a fork seat. This can also happen when the stirrups are the wrong length. When they are too short, the rider's leg has too much angle and her muscles cramp—a hard calf muscle can quickly make her horse dull to the leg. They also put the rider too far back in the saddle in a chair seat with the knees shoved forward and up and the lower legs too far forward. The rider will not be able to follow the movements of the horse with an elastic spine because the incorrect stirrup length causes her to round her back.

On the other hand, stirrups that are too long cause a fork seat. The rider's weight tips too much over the thighs and away from the seat and she will sit too far forward in the saddle. The toes are often pointed down in an effort to stay in the stirrups. This often hollows the back, which hinders a soft move-ment in sync with the horse's movement because the pelvis is locked. This position also causes the rider to stiffen because she knows that she can neither sit nor give any aids. In this case, shorter stirrups help posi-tion the rider's weight onto the seat. A small problem in seat or posture can cause a dom-ino effect and a long list of seat errors.

You can find the correct stirrup length by letting your legs hang down and then lift-ing your toe to find a comfortable place in the stirrup. It shouldn't feel as though you have to constantly stretch your legs in order to keep your feet in the stirrups. But it should not feel as if you have to pull your knee up to reach the stirrup.

The stirrup shouldn't make your ankle stiff or cause you to push down hard on the stirrup. When this happens, the stirrup is too short. Your foot should rest softly in the stirrup so that it has a little support. Imag-ine someone putting a hand on the stirrup under your foot—try not to squash the hand.

Longe lessons and dressage lessons in a jumping or multi-purpose saddle are not rec-ommended because the seat/leg position in these saddles is very different from that of a classical dressage saddle. This makes learn-ing the art of riding unnecessarily difficult for a young rider.

Experience has taught me that saddles with a solid tree provide better stability for riders than saddles without a tree or with a flexible tree, which make it especially diffi-cult to develop a quiet seat. The horse experi-ences the mistakes and bouncing of the rider in his back without the protection of the tree.

When a saddle sits well on the horse and fits the rider then it is practice, practice, and still more practice. Repeatedly selling and buying new saddles, as I have often done, does not lead to sitting better or the horse moving better. Don't fall for this! Riding is the most difficult of arts and requires many long years of intensive training, not just on the horse but also on the ground, to contin-ually work on improving your body posture and coordination so that you can finally cut a good figure on a horse. You can't buy the art of riding!

## A Quiet Atmosphere

This is very important if you want to concentrate on learning. A beginner is physically and mentally so challenged during her first riding lessons that the environment can negatively influence her. She must learn technique and feeling at the same time, which require calm surroundings. Other horses and riders, children crying, and dogs barking, can make learning more difficult or even impossible. A riding arena near pastures where horses are running around doesn't contribute to a quiet learning atmosphere: the danger is great that the horse will also get excited and the student unnecessarily frightened. Keep an eye out for a riding barn, preferably with an indoor riding arena, where you can be taught undisturbed and especially at times of day when there is not a lot going on.

The creation of an appropriate atmosphere is the responsibility of the owner and trainer of a riding stable. Look for a trainer that doesn't constantly yell loudly, cause nervousness, and make things tense. Choose one that is self-controlled and works quietly. Barns with politeness, respect, and definite rules assure you of smooth and safe traffic in the riding arena. Unfortunately, there are few of them.

You can also contribute to your riding lesson being a special experience of intense learning and a time of peace: leave your cell phone in the car. It should be possible to be unreachable for an hour.

Plan for enough time and try to not go to the barn frazzled. If possible, arrive an hour before your lesson time so that you can quietly watch other riders or spend time with the horse (your four-legged instructor).

## A Suitable Riding Outfit

A lot has already been written on this subject in innumerable books, so I would like to briefly make the points that are important to me concerning riding attire. A basic requirement is appropriate boots that are safe and won't get stuck in the stirrup. Jodhpur boots are appropriate footwear for jodhpur pants that give the rider a close contact feel to the horse's body. But tall boots give the beginner more security and make for a quieter leg: it is much more difficult to keep the leg quiet when wearing jodhpurs and jodhpur boots instead of breeches and tall riding boots.

On the subject of riding pants, there are innumerable styles, but the most important thing is that there are no seams that can dig into you. Anyone who has had a wide impression of a seam on the inside of the thigh or the knee after a riding lesson will appreciate this.

Breeches with leather or one of the new artificial seats improve "stick" in the saddle and encourage a more secure seat. These are good for beginners. Notice the cut of the pants at the knee—sometimes pants are cut too narrow and restrict bend in the knee. When you are trying on pants in the store, check that you can squat and bend your knees without the pants pressing on the knee. When squatting, also notice if the pants gap behind and squeeze you at the waistband in front. Unfortunately, this is a common design problem in ladies' breeches.

When the waistband sticks out behind it affects the appearance of your back and also just plain doesn't look good. Either find breeches that fit better, or keep the pants from sticking out behind by wearing a belt.

Avoid having loose change or keys with you. They can make a noise that will irritate the horse (and the rider) and consequently don't belong when you are on a horse.

Don't wear scarves or billowing shawls. They can come undone and slip—in the worst cases under your seat or the saddle. A sensitive horse could easily spook when he suddenly sees a blowing shawl out of the corner of his eye.

For the riding instructor to correct your posture, he must be able to see your silhouette. Wear body-hugging clothes and avoid sloppy T-shirts or your favorite baggy sweater. Tops with hoods are also not ideal because the instructor can't evaluate the back, especially your shoulder line, and they take away from the elegance of the rider.

Everyone must decide for herself about wearing a safety vest. With some models, it is very difficult for the riding instructor to see the line of the back, making it more difficult to correct for straight posture. A riding helmet should be required. I also recommend wearing riding gloves.

## Instruction on the Longe

Someone who hasn't ever sat on a horse before is generally busy enough with just staying up there and keeping her body under control. According to my experience, she can't manage to also guide the horse. Consequently, lessons on the longe are a good idea. Driving and steering the horse will be in competent hands, and the new rider can fully concentrate on her seat. Feeling the movement of the horse and gradually relaxing into it helps the student to feel more relaxed and calm. The riding instructor must help the beginner with this by teaching her to relax while paying attention that the student is maintaining even and deep breathing. Only then can the trainer influ-

*On the longe: the posting trot being ridden with correct posture.*

ence her seat and body posture. Just as for the horse, relaxation is the basis for learning to ride.

When the beginner is able to sit correctly and is relaxed at the walk, she can begin to trot. Begin work on the posting trot. The student must learn to stand in the saddle from the knees, without bringing her feet out of the stirrups, otherwise her whole leg will swing and her heel will be brought up every time she stands up.

The rider's upper body should be taken forward a little during the post, because the horse is moving forward. If she is too vertical going up, she can be left behind the movement when she comes back down to the saddle. This must be avoided because it hinders the horse's freedom of movement. Muscular strength must prevent sliding back in the saddle and the rider should never allow herself to fall down into the saddle because it is hard on the horse's back. She should

softly sit down on the saddle and lift back up after making soft contact with the saddle. Although the young rider working on the longe doesn't need reins, she should keep her hands in riding position in order to practice developing hands that are independent of other movements her body makes. This means that when standing up in the posting trot the hands should not be raised up. Since our longeing horse is well schooled, the rider can concentrate moving up and down as if

to a metronome and feel the rhythm of the trotting horse. It can help the student find the right tempo when the riding instructor counts out loud, because there should be a short pause in the air and not in the saddle at the posting trot.

Even in these first attempts at riding the trot, it is easy to see who is athletic and has sufficient body strength and coordination and who is deficient in this regard. The riding instructor should talk about this and give the student exercises to do at home to improve her physical fitness from the ground.

Next, the student begins to practice the sitting trot. This isn't something that can be accomplished in a few longeing lessons because sitting the trot with suppleness requires many years of training. But longe lessons provide an important foundation in the process of learning to follow the movement of the horse's back at the trot. At the begin-

ning, it is helpful for the student to hang on to the front of the saddle with one hand, and the back of the saddle with the other, so that she can pull herself deep into the saddle and practice moving her pelvis with the horse. Otherwise, she will try to clutch with her legs, which makes it harder to stay on the seat and shoves her out of the saddle, thus making sitting the trot impossible. Having the hands on the front and back of the saddle requires a slight twist of the upper body, which has to

*The correct position for mounting a horse: The snaffle rein and the whip are in the left hand.*

be accepted at the beginning. I recommend changing up having the inside hand on the front of the saddle and then the outside hand on the front. In this way, the upper body is turned more to the inside of the arena and then more to the outside. It is critical that the seat remains deep in the saddle and the rider lets her legs be loose instead of clamping onto the horse.

The rider should gradually let go with one hand and see if she can continue to trot and sit well. If that works, she should try to take both hands off the saddle. Finally, she brings the hands into riding position as if she were holding the reins and tries to remain still even though she is continuing to trot. What I've written here in a few lines is not the program for a single longe lesson, but requires many

lessons. When the riding student can hold herself fairly well on the horse and begins to follow the movement, she can begin to work on the correct seat and to correct her posture.

In order to achieve a good seat, a rider needs many gymnastic exercises. Circling the arms, turning the trunk, and circling the toes are just a few examples to help the student coordinate her body while mounted and

*Mounting correctly: The right hand grabs across the saddle.*

*A horse must stand absolutely still when being mounted. Here, the right leg is being taken over the croup correctly. The rider mustn't touch the horse with her foot.*

achieve good security in the saddle. A good riding instructor knows many such exercises and chooses them according to the physical need of the student. Our well-schooled longeing horse tolerates these gymnastic exercises without becoming insecure or, above all, changing tempo, rhythm, or carriage. In this way, the school horse gives a great deal to the beginning rider to help her learn the high art of riding securely and correctly. Ideally, a longeing horse doesn't have gaits that are too huge that would be very difficult for the student.

Along with work at the trot, the canter is practiced. Again, I like the rider to hold the saddle with two hands, one in front and one behind. From the very beginning, the exaggerated pushing with the seat at the canter must be avoided. Swinging the upper body and the pelvis from back to front disturbs the horse in the back and isn't a pretty sight. The rider should merely accept and follow the canter stride in the pelvis. It is helpful if she thinks more about "up and down" instead of "from back to front" so that this idea of "wiping" the saddle doesn't even get started. Later, gymnastic exercises are also important in order to develop an independent and supple seat.

Riding with no hands and no stirrups is a basic requirement for transitioning to riding instruction off the longe. The student must be able to stop the horse on the longe with her seat only, that is, without taking up the reins. In this way, she gets an idea of what she can achieve with her seat and will try to use it more effectively. Positive reinforcement from the instructor will encourage her to regard her hands as a sensitive accessory. She should never start thinking that the hands do most of the work or that they are there to help her stay on the horse's back.

Riding lessons on the longe should be continued now and then for the first several years, even when the rider can, at last, ride off the longe. This helps the rider to continually improve her seat and posture errors, which can creep back for all of us.

*Mounting incorrectly: The horse can reach the rider with his hind leg should he become frightened.*

## Brief Discussion of Mounting and Dismounting

For the first longe lesson, you need to climb on the horse. A competent riding instructor will explain exactly how to do it. A rider can get into dangerous situations when mounting simply because she doesn't do it correctly. The horse should stand quietly and square. You should speak to him as you approach him and take up the reins until you feel a connection with the horse's mouth. Stand facing the back at the left shoulder of the horse. From this position, lift your left leg and put your foot in the stirrup while the right hand reaches over the saddle and grabs the right side of the seat so that the saddle isn't pulled to the side.

Jump slowly but powerfully from the ground, take your right leg carefully over the croup without touching the horse and put your right foot in the stirrup before you sit down. Then settle carefully into the saddle. Many riders plop down with their whole weight onto the saddle before they get their foot into the right stirrup. This can cause a horrible load on the horse's back and he will tense up in anticipation of the weight falling down on him. Spare him this and sit with respect for his back.

Only in this way will your horse stand still patiently and relaxed for the whole process. If you use a riding whip, it should be held in the left hand at the horse's shoulder—not in the right hand. Otherwise, you have to take it with you over the croup as you get on and the horse could see the whip out of the corner of his eye high on the right and spook. A common way of mounting is to stand next to the horse facing his head and put the left foot in the stirrup, but by so doing, the rider unavoidably leans against the horse's body or even his flank and a ticklish horse can reflexively kick forward with his hind leg and hit the person, usually in the hip. I have experienced bad accidents from mounting this way. If you fall from this position, you will end up with your head under the hind legs of the horse. I, therefore, advise every rider to stick with the old proven method because it is much safer to stand at the horse's shoulder.

Using a mounting block is without question good for the horse, the rider, and the saddle. But the horse must be trained to stand absolutely still and be used to the mounting block. I have seen accidents happen when the horse thrashes with his legs, gets a hind leg caught in a mounting block, and runs off with the rider who is caught between the wall and the horse.

Basically, the rider shouldn't be so non-athletic that she can't get on without a mounting block.

*A mounting block is a comfortable and advantageous aid for the horse and rider, but it requires a well-trained horse.*

Dismounting has its own issues if you haven't learned to do it correctly. Ideally, take both feet out of the stirrups before dismounting. Support yourself forward on the saddle with your hands and get down. With young or sensitive horses, you may need to keep a little rein contact. The horse should be on the centerline of the arena and not near the wall. Lift your leg high enough so you don't touch your horse with your toe on the croup. Leave your hands on the saddle and don't suddenly press on the mane. If you have a whip, put it in the left hand before dismounting so that it doesn't swing up over the croup, which could possibly startle your horse.

## Education in Riding Theory

Every rider should study to gain fundamental knowledge. In order to be able to understand the initial seat corrections, she must understand the equestrian lexicon. If you don't understand such simple things as "inside and outside" or "wrong lead," you will lose valuable time making corrections by thinking about interpretations of the words. After every riding lesson, read about the theory and how you should do things in order to better correct deficiencies in practice. If you are committed to learning theory, you will dramatically speed your development as a rider.

Obviously, the arena figures are part of this basic knowledge. Memorize them so you can better concentrate on the essential things in the riding lesson and not waste any time thinking about in what direction to ride. Riding instructors prefer to work with students that have a basic knowledge and who are prepared theoretically. The instructor feels such a student is serious about learning to ride, and the practical instruction is easier.

It is also important for the student to understand why many actions in the saddle must be done in a certain way and not in another way, and the consequences of doing things incorrectly for her as well as for the horse. This knowledge gives her significant motivation to do things correctly, much more so than a rider that doesn't understand anything about the impact of her mistakes.

Read about the aids for the various exercises over and over again and learn them well, so that giving the aids from the saddle will be successful. Ask your riding instructor what books he recommends for your stage of learning. When you read something that is unclear to you, ask your instructor about it and try to work this knowledge into your riding.

If the student wants to go beyond the level of merely "being a passenger" and "going along with the movement" and, instead, become effective with her seat, she should be encouraged to read the works of the old masters. Sometimes what they say is hard to understand and there is room for different interpretations, but only constant reading and diligent practice in the saddle will make a rider into a good rider, perhaps one day, even a master.

Re-reading a certain passage of text after many additional riding lessons can suddenly bring clarity and you understand what the author wanted to express. This brings further milestones in your development as a rider.

*Remember, the art of riding is the most difficult of all arts because it requires body, character, and mind!*

# INDEX

Page numbers in *italics* indicate illustrations.